The Pictorial History of the
Vietnam War

Jeremy Barnes

GALLERY BOOKS
An imprint of W.H. Smith Publishers Inc.
112 Madison Avenue
New York, New York 10016

A Bison Book

Published by Gallery Books
A Division of W H Smith Publishers Inc.
112 Madison Avenue
New York, New York 10016

Produced by
Bison Books Corp.
15 Sherwood Place
Greenwich, CT 06830

ISBN 0-8317-6897-5

Printed in Spain

10 9 8 7 6 5 4 3 2 1

Page 1: *A CH-53 Sea Stallion
helicopter resupplies US Marines on
Hill 619 south of Danang.*

Pages 2–3: *Marines in the hills
outside Danang.*

Pages 4–5: *An A-7E Corsair II
being launched from the USS
Constellation in the South China
Sea.*

Following pages: *Viet Minh troops
march into Hanoi as French troops
leave the city by another route in
October 1954.*

CONTENTS

PART I
The Roots of War

Vietnam Through 1945

From its first recorded history to the present, Vietnam has been circumscribed by changing relationships to its giant neighbor to the north, China. We learn from Chinese chronicles of a distinct group called the Nam Viet, 'Southern People,' formed from Austronesian and Mongolian stock during the first millenium BC. In 111 BC, the Chinese burned the capital of Nam Viet and conquered the country; it would remain under Chinese rule for the next 1000 years, during which the subject people readily absorbed much of the sophisticated political organization and culture of their rulers. Nonetheless, there remained in the Nam Viet a fierce and ineradicable passion for independence and a strong opposition to assimilation by foreigners, the spirit called *Doc Lap*. That drive toward integrity achieved its object in AD 939, when the Nam Viet defeated the Chinese

But by the beginning of the 20th century, the high tide of Western colonialism had passed. The Japanese victory over Russia in 1905 gave new hope to the peoples of the East; in Vietnam, as elsewhere, the seeds of independence began to sprout. In the Versailles Peace Conference that followed World War I in 1919, a young French-educated nationalist named Nguyen Ai Quoc – 'Nguyen the Patriot' – presented an eight-point program for Vietnamese independence to President Woodrow Wilson. Nguyen hoped his program would arouse American ideals of freedom and self-determination but the proposal was ignored. It was the first of many times that America would disappoint the man who would eventually call himself Ho Chi Minh: 'Ho the Enlightened.'

Ho was a man obsessed with one goal – the independence and unification of Vietnam. In 1910 he had left his homeland for 30 years of wandering that would take him to France, Russia, and the United States; during those years he wrote and worked tirelessly for his cause. In 1930 he founded the Indochinese Communist Party and thereafter studied revolutionary theory and tactics with Mao Zedong in China. Finally, in 1941, Ho returned to his homeland, where he led the League for the Independence of Vietnam, called the Viet Minh, in fighting the Japanese, who controlled the country after France fell to the Germans. Commanding Ho's forces was General Vo Nguyen Giap, who was destined to lead the Vietnamese Communist armies in two more great struggles.

The aim of the Viet Minh during World War II was to rid Vietnam of both the Japanese and the French. With the aid of support from the Chinese Communists and the United States (by way of the OSS), their guerrilla war kept the Japanese off

Left: *Bao Dai, hereditary emperor of Vietnam, who remained the country's ruler in name only under both the French and the Japanese until the partition of Vietnam.*

Above: *The charismatic Vietnamese Communist leader Ho Chi Minh, who dedicated his life to the independence and unification of Vietnam.*

armies and became an independent state.

The next 900 years are called *nam-tien*, the March to the South, during which the Vietnamese people spread slowly along the coast until they reached the Mekong Delta. Around 1407 the Chinese reconquered the country, only to be expelled again in 1427, when the Vietnamese resumed their movement southward. In 1527 a long period of north-south conflict began that divided the country until it was reunited in 1802 by General Nguyen Anh, who became Emperor Gia Long.

General Anh's victory was accomplished with the help of a French missionary. Such missionaries had been in the country since the early 17th century, and over the years French influence had triumphed over that of other foreign powers who were sporadically interested in Vietnam. In the history of colonialism, missionaries often preceded conquering armies: the French seized Danang in 1857 and pushed on to take Saigon and Hanoi in subsequent years.

By 1867 Southern Vietnam was a French colony under the name Cochin China; an 1883 Treaty of Protectorate completed the French takeover. Discarding the name Vietnam, the new rulers further divided the country into Tonkin in the north and Annam in the center. The French had to suppress a popular uprising in 1885, and the late 19th century was marked by a dozen years of slaughter, under the euphemism of 'pacification,' in Tonkin. By the 1890s the French had achieved iron control of the entire area: they ruled Cambodia, Laos, and all three divisions of Vietnam, shrewdly exploiting internal ethnic and political rivalries to contain threats to their 'Indochinese Union.' In 1932 the French installed hereditary Emperor Bao Dai on the throne. For several decades this powerless sovereign would be a political football for the forces struggling for control of the country.

General Vo Nguyen Giap created the first platoon of the North Vietnamese Army with 34 men in 1944.

Above: *Vietnamese gunners fire on a French position with a 75mm weapon left behind by the Japanese.*

Left: *The newly appointed US envoy to China, General George C Marshall (left), visits Chinese Nationalist leader Chiang Kai-shek and Madame Chiang at Nanking in 1945. Four years later, Chiang and his Nationalist followers would flee to Taiwan after Mao Zedong's successful communist revolution.*

Right: *Troops of the French Foreign Legion operate amphibious vehicles in the marshes south of Saigon during operations against the Viet Minh in 1950, midway through the seven-year war for Indochina.*

balance. Hopeful of American aid after the war, Ho entreated President Harry S Truman for continued support against the French. But the U.S. government, torn between opposition to communism and colonialism, did not reply. In March 1945 the beleaguered Japanese put Bao Dai back on the throne as a figurehead. He was deposed in August 1945 when the Japanese pulled out and the Viet Minh took over, although the latter retained the hapless emperor as 'supreme advisor.'

On 12 September 1945 came one of the most significant and poignant episodes of this century: in a ceremony at Hanoi, Ho Chi Minh proclaimed the Independent Democratic Republic of Vietnam (DRV). At his side stood officers of the American Office of Strategic Services (OSS), the clandestine warfare service, who believed that only Ho had the power to lead an independent country. Ho's declaration began with a quotation from the American Declaration of Independence: 'All men are created equal, and . . . are endowed by their Creator with certain unalienable Rights, [And] among these are Life, Liberty, and the Pursuit of Happiness.' Just over a week later, French General Jacques Philippe Leclerc landed in Saigon with his own declaration: 'We have come to reclaim our inheritance.' The struggle that ensued would last for almost 10 years.

France Fights to Hold On

When negotiations between Vietnam and France made little progress, the violence escalated quickly: in November 1946, French troops swept through Haiphong to 'pacify' the city. In the process between 1000 and 6000 Viet Minh and civilians were killed. Then, on 19 December 1946, Ho's Democratic Republic of Vietnam launched its first attack on the French. Thus began the seven-year Indochina War.

From their northern base in Hanoi, the Viet Minh slowly expanded their guerrilla operations with widening popular support. Until 1949, the Saigon-based French easily contained the communists, while propping up Bao Dai on the throne once again. As each side solidified its military and political organizations, Vietnam was resundered along northern and southern lines.

The turning point for the Viet Minh came in 1949, when Mao Zedong's communists took over China. Now the ancient enemies, the Vietnamese and Chinese, became uneasy allies under the communist and anti-imperialist banner. Mao provided support for the resistance of his one-time pupil Ho Chi Minh, as did the Soviet Union. Inevitably, that tipped the balance for the United States, which was engaged in the Cold War: France's blatant colonialism left a bad taste in American mouths, but better that, Washington reasoned, than the victory of a communist group allied with China and the Soviet Union.

In May 1950, Secretary of State Dean Acheson announced that the United States would supply arms to the French. This sup-

port escalated until America was financing nearly half the cost of France's Indochinese War by the end of 1952 – the beginning of a very long escalation for the United States. But there was more than material aid; a commitment of military personnel soon followed. In August 1950 the first American Military Assistance Advisory Group (MAAG), 35 men, arrived in Vietnam to teach the French how to use their new weapons.

As months of fighting went by, however, neither American advisors nor a torrent of weapons could save the French; they were losing their grip on the country, especially in the North, and the French people were weary of what was called the 'dirty war.' In May 1953, the French entrusted command in Vietnam to one of their best generals, Henri Navarre, who arrived to proclaim of his prospects, 'Now we can see clearly, like light at the end of a tunnel.'

Navarre decided to throw out some bait to lure General Vo Nguyen Giap and his Viet Minh forces into the kind of large-scale battle that the French were certain they could win, one which would deal a devastating blow to the communists. The bait was to be a large garrison at Dien Bien Phu, in the North near the Laotian border. In placing his major force in a valley surrounded by hills, Navarre made several assumptions, all of them wrong. He did not believe the Viet Minh were a disciplined army capable of concentrating in superior numbers; he did not know the enemy now had modern Chinese artillery and Soviet anti-aircraft weapons and the ability to get the guns

Top left: *Chinese refugees who fled into Vietnam to escape the advancing communists cheer a representative of the Chinese Nationalist government at a camp on Phu Quoc Island (1950).*

Bottom left: *Zhou Enlai, who became premier of Communist China in 1949, presided over the uneasy alliance with the Vietnamese Communists led by Ho Chi Minh.*

Above: *French General Henri Navarre (left) inspects French and Vietnamese paratroopers at Dien Bien Phu in December 1953. As commander of French Union Forces in Indochina, Navarre sought a major victory against the Viet Minh from this base, recaptured from the communists only a month before.*

onto the heights; and he was confident that the garrison could be adequately supplied by air. For his part, General Giap could scarcely believe his luck: the French were sitting in the valley as at the bottom of a frying pan. If the Viet Minh could secure the heights, they would literally have the enemy at their feet.

At Dien Bien Phu, the French erected a formidable fortification ringed by nine strongpoints poetically named (it was said) for the current mistresses of commandant Christian de Castries. By early March 1954, the 11,000 defenders – which included a polyglot mixture of colonial troops and Foreign Legionnaires – knew Giap was preparing an attack. De Castries and his men were confident that their array of artillery, tanks, and strongpoints was impregnable. They could not know that the enemy

Left: *French troops involved in Operation Lorraine, a preliminary to the fight for Dien Bien Phu, radio their position from a North Vietnamese village during a halt.*

Bottom left: *French Union soldiers wounded during the Viet Minh attack on strongpoint Elaine, Dien Bien Phu: February 1954.*

Right: *Members of the communist People's Militia resupply Viet Minh troops around Dien Bien Phu. The popular forces would grow to 200,000 at the same time that General Giap built the North Vietnamese Army into a fighting machine of 350,000.*

Below: *The dreaded napalm bombs were introduced into Vietnam by the French. Here one bursts over Viet Minh trenches during 17 March fighting around Dien Bien Phu. Covered trenches in foreground shelter French defenders.*

had massed some 64,000 troops and, with incredible effort, had wrestled onto the heights dozens of howitzers, mortars, anti-aircraft guns, recoilless rifles and rocket launchers. In the thick jungle, French tanks would prove useless, and the enemy artillery was well camouflaged.

On 13 March the attack came. After heavy shelling, Giap threw human-wave assaults on strongpoints Gabrielle and Beatrice in the north; despite thousands of Viet Minh casualties, the positions were overrun in one day. Shortly thereafter, gunnery expert Colonel Charles Piroth, who had assured Navarre that 'no Viet Minh cannon will be able to fire three rounds before being destroyed by my artillery,' clutched a grenade to his chest and pulled the pin. A week later, the communists took strongpoint Anne-Marie and isolated Isabelle to the south.

The Eisenhower government, and the entire Western world, were thunderstruck at the reports. At a news conference, the president coined a phrase that became part of the language of international affairs. 'You have a row of dominoes set up, and you knock over the first one and what will happen to the last one is the certainty that it will go over very quickly. So you have the beginning of a disintegration.' Unwittingly, Eisenhower had postulated the doctrine that would drag America into intervention in Vietnam: the little country was perceived as the first domino that international communism was trying to push over in Southeast Asia.

At first the administration planned air strikes to aid the French, but pulled back when Britain refused to support the idea. The situation at Dien Bien Phu stabilized briefly on 10 April when a French counterattack drove the enemy from an area called 'the Hills' near the vital airstrip. General Giap, now in personal command of communist forces, took stock: the French had lost 2000 casualties and the garrison was clearly doomed, but the Viet Minh had squandered some 20,000 casualties with human-wave assaults. Now Giap decided on a change to conventional siege tactics, digging trenches and bunkers closer and closer to the French, slowly but inexorably choking off the garrison.

By 1 May the defensive perimeter at Dien Bien Phu had been reduced from its original 50 kilometers to less than 8; the 8000 remaining defenders (there had been 4000 airborne reinforce-

Main picture: *French Union Forces supported by tanks move toward a Viet Minh company south of Dien Bien Phu in late March 1954.*

Far left: *A French Union paratrooper watches dozens of French and Vietnamese comrades descend from the skies over Dien Bien Phu.*

Center, top and bottom: *Wounded French Union soldiers are evacuated by air to nearby Laos, as stretcher bearers search the perimeter at Dien Bien Phu for additional casualties.*

Left: *Both helicopters and light planes were employed to evacuate casualties from the besieged fortress, but they could not keep pace with the numbers of the wounded.*

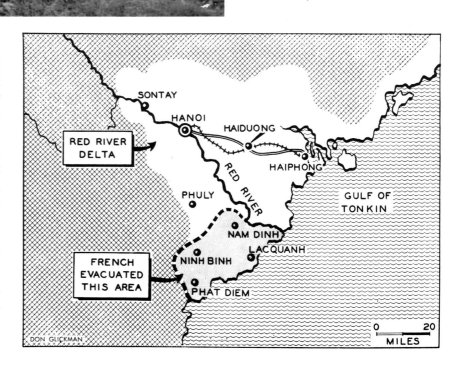

Top left: *French soldiers dash for cover in the wasteland around the doomed fortress: May 1954.*

Above: *French prisoners of war study the news from home.*

Left: *Exhausted prisoners leave Dien Bien Phu under guard.*

Below: *French withdrawal from the southern zone of the Red River Delta left more than 1600 square miles of a rich rice-producing area under communist control.*

ments) huddled under mortar fire within a circle of their dead. In places, enemy trenches were only yards from the defenders; supporting air strikes were ravaged by communist anti-aircraft fire and air drops of food and supplies often landed in enemy positions. The French had fought heroically, but there was no hope left.

Following a blistering hail of artillery fire and the detonation of tunnels dug into the French positions, the final communist assault came on 6 May, when waves of screaming Viet Minh troops poured into the garrison. On 7 May Colonel de Castries announced by radio that the enemy were at the door of his bunker. After 56 days, the Battle of Dien Bien Phu was finished. France had lost 2200 killed, over 6000 wounded, and 6000 taken prisoner; less than half the latter would survive captivity. General Giap had suffered severe losses – some 10,000 dead and 20,000 wounded, most of them in the human-wave attacks – but he had proved to the world that his guerrillas could inflict humiliating defeat on the army of a major power.

Negotiations and Divisions

When France and the Viet Minh met with seven other nations – including the United States, China and the Soviet Union – for negotiations at Geneva, Switzerland, in July 1954, the French came to the table as losers on the battlefield. The Geneva Accords, which officially ended the Indochina War, were yet another humiliation for the French, who had given independence to Laos and Cambodia in 1953. They were now about to lose Vietnam. The Accords called for a 'temporary' partition of the country at the 17th parallel, French withdrawal from the North, and communist control of the North and noncommunist control of the South pending nationwide elections in 1956 (which the Viet Minh were certain they would win). Secretly, the Viet Minh were outraged that in the negotiations the Chinese had pressured them into withdrawing from Laos and Cambodia and had even suggested leaving Vietnam permanently partitioned. In the long run, the Accords achieved a cease-fire but solved nothing; indeed, most were never signed.

As the conference finished, the US Military Assistance Advisory Group had 342 men in South Vietnam. American colonel Edward G Lansdale had arrived in the South in June to head the Saigon Military Mission, co-ordinating paramilitary operations against the communists. Fearful of a communist takeover, the Americans were gearing up for a secret war.

Bao Dai, still the figurehead leader of the South, selected Ngo Dinh Diem as the new prime minister. Diem was a dedicated

Top: *Ho Chi Minh visits with young members of the communist popular forces, to whom he was a hero, in the wake of victory over the French.*

Above: *John Foster Dulles, US Secretary of State under Eisenhower, was committed to the containment of communism at almost any price, even to 'the brink of war.'*

nationalist from an old mandarin family, and a Roman Catholic. After the Accords, a stream of nearly a million refugees poured from the North into the South, with help from the US Navy. Many of these refugees were Catholic, and they would help form the core of Diem's support. In November 1954, General Lawton Collins arrived in Saigon to 'co-ordinate the operation of all US agencies in that country.' He announced $100 million in American aid and stated that the United States would take charge of training the Vietnamese Army.

Diem began consolidating his power late in 1955, when he called for a referendum, rigged it elaborately with Lansdale's help, and thereby ousted Bao Dai and proclaimed a Republic of Vietnam with himself as president. By then, the forces that would eventually destroy Diem were already gathering. There was violent resistance by the private armies of the Dinh Xuyen, Cao Dai, and Hoa Hao sects, who had been armed and trained to fight the French by the Japanese during their wartime occupation of Vietnam. Diem's 'land reform' program would create discontent by appropriating land from the peasants and giving it to rich landowners. And Diem's increasing favoritism for the elite Catholic minority at the expense of the Buddhist majority aroused widespread resentment. In mid-1957 Diem visited the United States, where Eisenhower hailed him as Asia's 'miracle man.' But privately, the US government had already begun to fear that there would be no miracles, and that it was backing the wrong man.

Left: *Even as they were losing their hold on Indochina, the French demanded conscription of all men between the ages of 21 and 25 (April 1954).*

Left: *US Navy personnel on the Saigon River in 1953 salute HMS* Alert, *flagship of the Commander-in-Chief, Far East Station.*

Right: *President Dwight D Eisenhower welcomes Ngo Dinh Diem, president of the Republic of Vietnam, to Washington in May 1957.*

Left: *Residents of Haiphong wave the North Vietnamese flag – a yellow star on a red ground – as the communist militia enters the port in May 1955.*

Secret War and Turmoil

Diem's visit to America alerted the Viet Minh to the fact that the United States was moving in after the final French pullout in spring 1956. From the communist perspective, the country was in danger of exchanging one colonial power for another. Meanwhile, Diem had refused to hold the elections mandated by the Geneva Accords – because he knew the communists would win. Thus the Viet Minh turned to violence, initiating a program of sabotage, harassment, and murder; by the end of 1957, they had killed some 400 minor South Vietnamese officials. This terrorist campaign forced Diem into increasingly repressive measures as he attempted to contain the communist threat, but as the Viet Minh intended, these measures only alienated more peasants from the South Vietnamese government.

The terrorists did not neglect the US presence. On 22 October 1957, 13 Americans were wounded in three bombings of MAAG and US Information Service installations in Saigon. By that point, Hanoi had organized 37 armed companies to operate in the Mekong Delta, within South Vietnam. Two American soldiers became the first men killed during hostilities when guerrillas hit a MAAG compound in Bienhoa, near Saigon, on 8 July 1959. At the end of that year, the CIA intercepted a Hanoi directive ordering 'a new stage of the struggle,' a move into overt insurgency.

That new stage became operational with a vengeance in 1960. The communists moved men and material south down the Ho Chi Minh Trail (actually a network of trails) which ran through Laos near the western border of Vietnam and would become the lifeline of Hanoi's war effort. Assassinations of South Vietnamese officials escalated: 1200 in 1959, 4000 in 1961. In September 1959, communists ambushed two companies of South

Above: *CIA operative Col Edward G Lansdale was one of the people most responsible for the early US involvement in Vietnam. Between 1954 and 1956, he became a close advisor to Diem, whose power he helped to consolidate. During the early 1960s, he influenced President Kennedy with his demands for more support of the unpopular South Vietnamese president.*

Left: *French premier Pierre Mendès-France represented his nation at the Geneva Conference of 1954, during which Vietnam was divided.*

Above: *Two Vietcong suspects captured by ARVN Airborne Battalion members are held for questioning during a sweep to drive communist guerrillas from cover.*

Left: *A North Vietnamese unit operates US-made 75mm pack howitzers (1959). Communist weapons ranged from modern Soviet-supplied armaments to World War II-vintage guns abandoned by the Japanese. Captured US weapons were welcome additions to the North Vietnamese arsenal.*

Vietnamese soldiers, killing 12 of them and wounding others.

Attempting to respond, Diem began to appoint military men to administrative posts while continuing to neglect the desperate social and economic needs of the populace. Increasingly, he isolated himself from the people and came under the sway of his shadowy brother Ngo Dinh Nhu, who encouraged him to crack down on any opposition – especially from the Buddhists. The result was an upsurge in violent dissent: a peasant uprising in Ben Tre Province in January 1960, a coup attempt by a military faction in December.

At the end of 1960, Hanoi announced the formation of the National Front for the Liberation of the South, known as the National Liberation Front or NLF. This Hanoi-controlled coalition of South Vietnamese political and religious groups was dubbed the Vietcong (Vietnamese Communists, or VC) by Saigon in an effort to discredit it. By the end of the year, as the social and political climate of the South approached chaos, some 4500 Vietcong had infiltrated the area. The new American president, John F Kennedy, would have a great deal of anxiety about a country most Americans had never heard of in 1960.

Kennedy Commits to War

In his inaugural address, President Kennedy proclaimed that the United States would 'pay any price, bear any burden, meet any hardship, support any friend, oppose any foe, to assure the survival and success of liberty.' Clearly, Southeast Asia was one of the places he had in mind. Eisenhower had warned Kennedy that communist insurgency threatened neutral Laos and that the situation might call for American military intervention.

In March 1961 a US reconnaissance plane was shot down over Laos, its pilot another of the unheralded American casualties of covert warfare. Soon afterward, Walt Rostow, a senior White House advisor and specialist on Southeast Asia, proposed to Kennedy that the time had come for 'gearing up the whole Vietnam operation.' To that end, Rostow made several suggestions that were implemented: Vice-President Lyndon Johnson was sent to Vietnam in May to meet with Diem, whom he called 'the Churchill of Asia'; US support to the Army of the Republic of South Vietnam (ARVN) was increased; and Diem was pressured again to enact reforms and broaden his political base.

After the April debacle of the Kennedy-sanctioned invasion of Cuba's Bay of Pigs, and an unsatisfactory summit meeting with blustering Soviet Premier Nikita Khrushchev in June, the president decided that South Vietnam was an arena in which to make good his declaration that the United States would pay any

Above: President John F Kennedy outlines the situation in Southeast Asia during a press conference on 23 March 1961, shortly before he doubled US troops in South Vietnam to 1200.

In his 1961 inaugural address, Kennedy made far-reaching pledges to 'support any friend, oppose any foe, to assure . . . liberty.' His use of South Vietnam as an exemplar of this policy would haunt his successors and the nation.

A camouflaged youth takes part in a Civil Defense Group training exercise supervised by US advisors in Thua Thien. In the wake of General Maxwell Taylor's 1961 recommendation for a 'massive joint effort' to support South Vietnamese efforts against the Vietcong, dozens of such camps sprang up in the South, while the number of American military advisors and Special Forces personnel increased steadily.

price to assure liberty. However, the authoritarianism, incompetence, and corruption of the Diem government was a major obstacle to Kennedy's attempts to paint the region as a bastion of democracy. The internal uncertainty and turmoil that would mark the Kennedy administration's relationship with Vietnam reflected the turmoil of Diem's rule.

The general trend in 1961 was a piece-by-piece increase of American personnel and weapons. In May Kennedy sent 400 Special Forces troops and 100 other military advisors to Vietnam to supplement the 685 advisors already in place. He also ordered the formation of a South Vietnamese clandestine warfare unit under the direction of the CIA and Special Forces. Deeply involved in this 'First Observation Group' was Colonel Edward G Lansdale, whose zest for secret operations and indifference to political subtleties would make him the model for the title character of two novels – *The Ugly American* and *The Quiet American*.

After a visit to Vietnam in October, close Kennedy advisor General Maxwell Taylor pressed for a 'massive joint effort' to help the South fight the Vietcong. Kennedy hesitated on the brink of major troop commitments, but did order in more troops – they would number 16,000 within two years – military aircraft, and two Army helicopter companies with their crews. On a visit to the Special Warfare Center at Fort Bragg in September, Kennedy had been impressed with the new unit's potential for counterinsurgency operations. Perhaps he hoped that these 'Green Berets' could keep America from having to fight a conventional war in Southeast Asia.

By the end of 1961, the Kennedy administration had upped the ante of American commitment enormously. 'Operation Farm Gate' bombers were authorized to fly combat missions if there were a token South Vietnamese aboard. A massive airborne defoliation operation had been ordered; the MAAG force in the country had reached 3200; American flyers were engaging in extensive reconnaissance missions and training the South Vietnamese Air Force; over $200 million in US aid to Vietnam had been disbursed during the year. In the same period, 14 Americans had been killed or wounded in combat.

Above: *A Vietnamese Air Force A-26 bomber armed with two napalm bombs and a rocket pod under each wing. Eight .50 caliber machine guns are in the nose.*

Left: *A Montagnard hut of bamboo and thatch houses a relocated mountain family within the limits of the Vietnam Special Forces Camp at An Diem.*

Deepening Engagement

By 1962 it was no longer a matter of South Vietnam fighting scattered bands of Vietcong guerrillas; now, as Diem observed, it was a 'real war' against an enemy who 'attacks us with regular units fully and completely equipped.' Each government, Ho Chi Minh's in Hanoi and Diem's in Saigon, proclaimed itself the only legal government of the country and the only means of re-unification. The Americans, involved at every level of military operations and keeping a close eye on political doings as well, were inexorably becoming enmeshed both on the battlefield and in the machinations of the South Vietnamese government – when bullets flew or coups were plotted, Americans were often present.

In January 1962 the US Air Force began the defoliation program called 'Operation Ranch Hand,' designed to expose the roads and trails through the jungle used by the Vietcong. Over the next nine years, US planes would dump some 19 million gallons of herbicides over one-fifth of Vietnam and parts of Laos. This controversial operation was destined to have little

success in impeding enemy movements. The first Operation Farm Gate mission took off on 13 January, as US fighter-bombers struck Vietcong around an ARVN outpost; 229 such missions followed in the next two weeks. The 39th Signal Battalion, the first regular US ground unit in the country, arrived in February. That same month, the first American helicopter was downed by hostile fire.

Increasing US commitment was reflected in a reorganization of command. General Paul D Harkins was installed in Saigon to head the Military Assistance Command, Vietnam (MACV), which would now supervise the activities of MAAG. In an effort to obscure the extent of US operations, President Kennedy described them as 'training missions,' and added, 'we have not sent combat troops in [the] generally understood sense of the word.'

The ARVN mounted its first major counteroffensive against the Vietcong in late March. This 'Operation Sunrise' was an attempt to strike the communists in Binh Duong Province, 35

Top left: *A Vietnamese Army tank patrols the streets of Saigon after the March 1962 attempt on the life of President Diem.*

Above: *Both men and women were trained for South Vietnam's Civil Defense Guard, seen here drilling at Hao Cain.*

Left: *A female member of the Vietcong captured by the ARVN in 1962. Her hands are bound with the communist flag.*

miles north of Saigon. The Vietcong melted away as the ARVN began to build 'strategic hamlets' – fortified stockades to which peasants were forcibly relocated. Diem and his brother Nhu pursued this strategic hamlet program ruthlessly, with the intent of denying the Vietcong their necessary contact with the people. The result was exactly the opposite: after being evicted from their villages and corralled into stockades by the ARVN, peasants were far more sympathetic to the communists. (The program was abandoned in 1964.)

Each step-up in US operations brought with it an increase in casualties. A Farm Gate plane crashed on 11 February, killing nine US and South Vietnamese crew members. On 9 April two American soldiers were killed when the Vietcong ambushed an ARVN unit. Responding to casualty reports, Kennedy said, 'We cannot desist in Vietnam,' and sent more troops: a Marine helicopter unit arrived in April to join the three Army helicopter units carrying ARVN soldiers into battle. By May 1962, some 5000 US troops were in the country; the same month, 3000 Marines made a show of force in Thailand to discourage communist Pathet Lao troops from crossing the Laotian border into Thailand.

All these US efforts had no effect on a deteriorating situation. The government of Diem and Nhu pursued the disastrous strategic hamlet program and numerous complicated intrigues. After two frustrated South Vietnamese pilots bombed the presidential palace in February, the government itself became increasingly precarious. In a major ARVN offensive in Tay Ninh Province called 'Operation Morning Star,' 5000 troops claimed only 42 enemy casualties in a week of operations. US officials declared Morning Star a failure and disclaimed responsibility. After a week of global anxiety during October, when Kennedy pressured the Soviets into removing their missiles from Cuba, the administration turned its full attention to Vietnam and quickly sank even more deeply into the dilemmas of the situation as into quicksand.

Above: *A deep moat lined with bamboo stakes and encircled by barbed wire encloses South Vietnamese families forcibly relocated from their villages to deny the Vietcong shelter and support.*

Top right: *The bombing of the presidential palace in Saigon by dissident ARVN pilots (1962) was only one example of the turmoil within the Diem regime.*

Bottom right: *A South Vietnamese soldier destroys Vietcong propaganda uncovered during a raid in the Camau Peninsula.*

Left: *Commander Ivar A Johnson of the USS* Mahan *escorts President Diem through the ship, docked in Saigon in the fall of 1962.*

The Covert and Irregular War

Kennedy hoped to defeat the communists in Vietnam with American directed covert and irregular operations – guerrillas and infiltrators fighting their North Vietnamese counterparts. Central to these counterinsurgency efforts were the Special Forces, or Green Berets (whose distinctive headgear had been authorized by Kennedy himself) and a tangle of CIA operations. Later, when the American commitment increased into large conventional forces, the covert operations assumed a life of their own.

Kennedy's confidence in the Special Forces as the front line of counterinsurgency gave them a status unusual even for an elite unit. Many of the Green Berets were bilingual, having been trained to work closely with indigenous groups. They were a corps and a world unto themselves: highly trained, self-sufficient, and often associated with civilians in operations that were obscure to other military personnel. They had little contact with regular forces, and as a result were often viewed with suspicion by the majority, who had an ingrained distrust of such elite organizations.

The primary concern of the Green Berets was the *montagnard* (mountain) tribes around Pleiku. These primitive and fiercely independent highland people were traditionally despised by the lowland peasants and had little love for their countrymen of any political stripe. They were happy to exchange their spears and crossbows for modern weapons. The Green Beret-trained Civilian Irregular Defense Group (CIDG), consisting of *montagnards* and other ethnic and religious minorities, became an effective paramilitary force, but their operations were only a sideshow in the later full-scale American war. Early Green Beret efforts to train counterinsurgency and commando troops for the ARVN had little success. Eventually, the other services got into the guerrilla game – the Navy's Sea, Air and Land teams (SEALs) and the US Air Force Air Commandos. The latter formed a squadron nicknamed 'Jungle Jim,' which flew Operation Farm Gate combat missions in the early 1960s.

Above: *President Kennedy confers with Brigadier General William Yarborough, commandant of the Special Warfare Center at Fort Bragg, North Carolina, in 1961.*

Right: *Members of a Navy Sea, Air, Land (SEAL) team rappell from a hovering helicopter to set up a jungle ambush.*

Left: Montagnards *trained in commando operations by men of the US Special Forces patrol the hills around their outpost in search of Vietcong.*

Group' established in Vietnam in 1956; its 300 men trained South Vietnamese for a wide range of counterinsurgency projects. In 1961 Kennedy authorized expanding the group to 805 men and shifting the focus of activities from the South to the North.

Far left: *'Neutral' Laos became deeply involved in the Vietnam War when US Army advisors came into the country to train Laotian soldiers, one of whom is seen here in camouflage during a cover-and-concealment drill.*

Left: *Boobytraps and mines were a mainstay of covert and irregular warfare in Vietnam.*

Top right: *US infantrymen scatter into their landing zone to establish a defensive perimeter.*

CIA efforts were far more Byzantine in their complexity, their operations harder to trace and pin down. The agency would organize units for specific purposes and wait to see what happened: those that seemed to work were extended, those that seemed ineffective were redirected. Activities ranged from 'psywar' teams that pursued political-psychological objectives, to small commando hit squads, to full-fledged secret armies. One example is the euphemistically named 'First Observation

Other CIA efforts included the Program Evaluation Office, which pursued political and military operations in Laos. The most successful Laotian operation began in 1959, when the PEO sent Lieutenant Colonel Arthur 'Bull' Simons and a small US Special Forces White Star team to train Meo tribesmen in behind-the-lines guerrilla warfare. Over the next 10 years, this outfit grew to more than 40,000 men – the largest secret army in CIA history. They were a primary force in prevention of a Pathet Lao takeover during the 1960s. Supporting this and other operations – including some into Communist China – was Air America, a covert CIA airline.

In general, covert and irregular operations during the war had striking successes (notably among the American-trained units of tribesmen and other minorities) and dismal failures (like the strategic hamlet program). But their overall progress in fighting the communists mirrored that of the overt war – a long, slow downhill slide.

Left: *Kennedy and Vice-President Lyndon B Johnson proved the truth of the axiom that politics makes strange bedfellows. But whatever their personal differences, they presented a united front on the issue of US involvement in Vietnam.*

The Year of the Assassins

It was in 1963 that the tattered fabric of the Diem government unravelled, and the aftermath inevitably changed the nature and scope of American commitment. The year's fighting began ominously in January with the Battle of Ap Bac, in the Mekong Delta southeast of Saigon. There, 2500 well-armed ARVN troops, flown in on American helicopters with accompanying United States advisors and supported by armored and air units, were soundly defeated by some 400 Vietcong. They killed 65 ARVN and 3 Americans, wounded over 100, and downed or damaged 16 helicopters before slipping away with light casualties. It was a stunning demonstration of ARVN deficiencies in leadership and morale.

Violent political unrest followed this battlefield debacle. After a Diem provincial official ordered an attack on participants in a Buddhist holiday celebration that left 9 dead and 20 wounded, the Buddhists began a campaign of protest and resistance. They made up some 70 percent of the South Vietnamese population, as opposed to the 10 percent of Catholics who

dominated the government. Thus hatred of Diem's long-standing pro-Catholic policies was widespread.

In June came the first of the fiery protests that horrified the world. On a Saigon street, in the presence of press photographers, Buddhist monk Quang Duc immolated himself with gasoline in protest of the Diem regime. Other such suicides followed. There seemed no choice for Diem but to come to some rapprochement with the Buddhists; instead, he stalled, and in August secretly ordered an attack on temples and sanctuaries that killed and wounded hundreds. Madame Nhu, wife of Diem's brother and self-styled First Lady of Vietnam, crowned the horror by calling the immolations 'barbeques' and offering to supply matches. It was the supreme example of how isolated and arrogant the South Vietnamese government had become.

In August newly appointed ambassador to South Vietnam Henry Cabot Lodge arrived in Saigon. Shrewdly, Kennedy had named a former Republican political opponent to the post to demonstrate bipartisan support for administration policies.

Lodge found the government in shambles and much of the population demonstrating violently in the streets. Moreover, as CIA operative Lucien Conein informed Lodge, a group of generals were plotting a coup against Diem under the leadership of Generals Tran Van Dong and Duong Van Minh, who was called 'Big Minh.' In light of the near-chaos in the country, Lodge began urging Washington to support the coup.

At that point, the efforts of administration officials in Washington and Saigon also fell into disarray, with various channels working at cross-purposes. There was no question about continued American involvement: a campaign by French president Charles De Gaulle to make Vietnam neutral was rejected by the United States. In October 1963, the glamorous Madame Nhu toured the United States in an effort to create support for the Diem government. She was followed by her father, a Catholic who had shaved his head like a Buddhist monk to protest the repressions, and who bitterly contested the defiant speeches of his daughter. The American public found it all rather amusing.

The imperative question now was what to do about Diem and Nhu, and whether to encourage the coup. It was a sobering prospect for the United States – active support of a violent change of government in another country. Among those rejecting the plot were MACV commander General Paul Harkins, who convinced Kennedy aide General Maxwell Taylor that it was potentially disastrous. Conein and Lodge, meanwhile, gave full support to the dissident generals. Kennedy waffled, now encouraging the coup and now trying to put it off; his last word to Lodge on 29 October, as the coup was about to begin, was to suppress it. Lodge simply pocketed the order.

On the morning of 1 November, Lodge paid a courtesy call on Diem, knowing that the generals were massing their forces for a coup later that day. Around noon, CIA agent Conein strapped

Left: *A rapid series of events shocked the nation and the world on 22 November 1963, when President Kennedy was assassinated during a motorcade through Dallas, Texas. At top, seconds before the shots rang out, the Kennedys are riding through the city with Texas Governor John Connally and Mrs Connally. At center, onlookers take cover after the president is shot, as the motorcade breaks up and the presidential car speeds toward the hospital.*

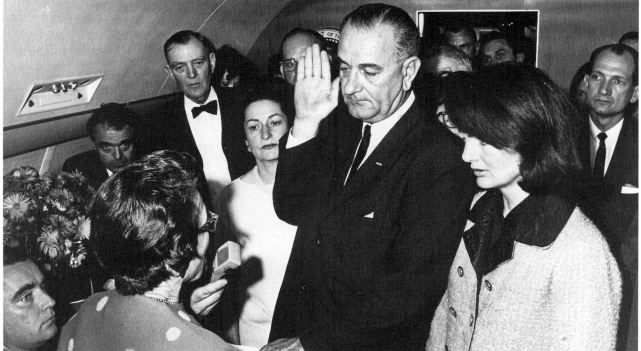

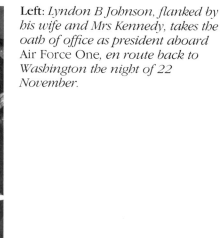

Left: *Lyndon B Johnson, flanked by his wife and Mrs Kennedy, takes the oath of office as president aboard* Air Force One, *en route back to Washington the night of 22 November.*

on a Western-style revolver, picked up a suitcase containing $40,000 for the insurgents, and notified his superiors that the coup was beginning. Events followed fast: the palace was surrounded by dissident troops, some key military leaders were shot, others went over to the insurgents. Escaping to a hideout in Saigon, Diem and Nhu bargained with the generals by telephone, finally receiving assurances of safe conduct into exile. But after a US-built armored personnel carrier picked up Diem and Nhu on 2 November, they were riddled with bullets on orders of Big Minh. Nonetheless, at the end of the day Lodge called the generals into his office to congratulate them, then cabled Kennedy that prospects were bright. For his part, Kennedy was horrified at the assassinations.

The confusions and uncertainties of Kennedy administration policy ended on 22 November 1963, when the president was himself assassinated in Dallas by Lee Harvey Oswald. This tragedy left to his successor Lyndon Johnson the problems of the conflict and to the speculations of history the question of whether Kennedy would have gone on to full-scale war in Vietnam.

LBJ Takes Charge

The end of 1963 saw Lyndon Baines Johnson at the head of the American government and the Revolutionary Military Committee under Big Minh in control of South Vietnam. All had acceded to office by way of assassination, but in Vietnam the killers ran the government.

Big Minh pledged to pursue democracy; President Johnson pledged to continue Kennedy's support of South Vietnam and sent Defense Secretary Robert McNamara into the country to make a report. McNamara, who had been Kennedy's Secretary of Defense, was an enthusiastic advocate of air operations.

Top: *Maxwell D Taylor, US Ambassador to Vietnam, addresses newly arrived American troops as General William C Westmoreland looks on.*

Above: *Westmoreland inspects troops at Vam Lang on an orientation tour as the newly appointed commander in Vietnam.*

Right: *The wreckage of US B-57 jet bombers litters the site of the Bien Hoa Airbase in the wake of a Vietcong attack.*

Former president of the Ford Motor Company, he was to run the war as if it were largely a statistical matter of production, supply, and body counts. After viewing the situation in late 1963, McNamara was publicly upbeat, but pessimistic in his report to Johnson: 'Conflicts [within the government] could develop serious schisms, precipitate further dissensions and coup attempts all of which will affect the war effort against the VC.' He concluded, 'There are more reasons to doubt the future of the effort under present programs . . . than there are reasons to be optimistic about the future of our cause in South Vietnam.'

For both Johnson and McNamara, the answer to the problems of 'present programs' was to add new programs. But it had to be done discreetly; an election was coming up in the United States and Johnson had to avoid alarming doves by being too warlike or offending hawks by vacillation. But his direction was already mapped out: 'Just let me get elected,' he told the Joint Chiefs of Staff in late 1963, 'and you can have your war.'

In January Johnson approved Oplan 34A, which heated up clandestine operations. It ordered spy flights, 'psywar' teams, and sabotage in the North and Navy strikes on North Vietnamese coastal operations. American pilots would bomb communist positions in Laos from planes bearing Laotian Air Force insignia. Finally, US Navy destroyers would patrol the Gulf of Tonkin under the codename 'DeSoto Mission.' In June 1964, General Harkins was replaced as Military Assistance Command, Vietnam chief by General William Westmoreland.

Left: *During his brief tenure as chief of state in South Vietnam, Phan Khac Suu, flanked by Generals Duong Van Minh (left) and Nguyen Khanh, commander-in-chief of the ARVN, reviews a National Independence Day parade.*

Below: By the summer of 1964, General Nguyen Khanh was at the head of the unstable government in Saigon. During this period of military coups and countercoups, ARVN tanks were being called 'voting machines.'

Oplan 34A was implemented amid continuing political tumult in the South. In late January 1963, the military junta was toppled in a bloodless coup led by Major General Nguyen Khanh; the government would turn over three more times during the year, each regime as corrupt and incompetent as the one before it. In Saigon, ARVN tanks were being called 'voting machines.' The United States made futile attempts to bolster each successive regime. Meanwhile, VC terrorists took a steady toll of civilians and government officials, and the demoralized ARVN made no progress on the battlefield.

As Johnson geared up his election campaign, trying to appear dovish by comparison with his saber-rattling Republican challenger Barry Goldwater, new threats accumulated in strife-torn Southeast Asia. Prince Sihanouk of Cambodia began to insist

stridently on his country's neutrality, despite the fact that the Vietcong had sanctuaries in Cambodia. The communist Pathet Lao went on the offensive in neutral Laos after Prince Souvanna Phouma succeeded in molding a US-supported coalition government. And border incidents multiplied between ARVN forces and communists using Laos and Cambodia for sanctuary.

Within the Johnson administration, the consensus was clear that American military might was the answer to all these prob-

lems. Despite explicit public denials by Johnson, plans were being developed to bomb North Vietnam. Advisor Walt Rostow suggested that the president seek grounds for a Congressional resolution empowering him to wage war, and in May Deputy Secretary of Defense William Bundy wrote a draft of such a document. In August 1964, that draft would become the Tonkin Gulf Resolution – on the basis of shaky, if not downright specious, evidence.

Above: *Secretary of Defense Robert S McNamara visits units of the US Military Assistance Command in Vietnam. On his right is General Lyman L Lemnitzer, chairman of the Joint Chiefs of Staff.*

Left: *Young Vietcong prisoners are guarded by ARVN soldiers in a Vietnam port. The coastal cities were heavily infiltrated by communist soldiers from North Vietnam.*

PART II

America Commits to War

The Tonkin Gulf Incident

In 1964 the Johnson administration had not declared openly its decision to go to war in Vietnam, but it was actively planning in that direction. A provoking incident would not be hard to find, given steadily mounting communist operations and the number of American troops coming into the line of fire – the United States had 16,500 servicemen in the country by the end of 1963, and during that year the troops suffered 489 casualties, a fourfold increase over the previous year. As it happened, however, the incident that unleashed administration plans occurred not on land but at sea, in the Gulf of Tonkin.

By July 1964, the DeSoto Mission, part of the Oplan 34A clandestine operations, was well underway in the Gulf under Admiral Ulysses Grant Sharp, Jr, Honolulu-based Navy commander for the Pacific. He ordered the carrier *Ticonderoga* into the Gulf with its supporting force; the destroyer *Maddox*, under captain John J Herrick, sailed from Japan to pursue radio eavesdropping on the North Vietnamese.

On 30–31 July, six South Vietnamese PT boats bombarded enemy installations on two islands in the Tonkin Gulf, Hon Me and Hon Ngu. On 2 August, the *Maddox*, patrolling the area, intercepted a North Vietnamese radio signal mentioning 'military operations'; Captain Herrick wondered if some sort of retaliatory raid were being prepared. Early that afternoon, three enemy patrol boats appeared and launched torpedoes. Herrick opened fire from the *Maddox* and requested air support from the *Ticonderoga*. The torpedoes failed to connect and Herrick's fire, plus strafing by US Crusader jets, sank one of the communist boats and crippled the others. It was all over in 20 minutes, and the US ships were ordered to withdraw. Hearing the report, Johnson rejected for the moment the idea of reprisals.

The Joint Chiefs of Staff were less inclined to wait and see; they put US combat troops on alert, sent fighter-bombers to the area, and ordered the carrier *Ticonderoga* and another destroyer, the *Turner Joy*, to sail into the Gulf: US ships were ordered right up to the edge of North Vietnamese waters. As Captain Herrick knew, this constituted a gauntlet thrown down before the communists. The situation was extremely tense. The North Vietnamese government had already made a formal accusation against the United States as perpetrator of the island raids.

On the evening of 4 August, as the *Maddox* and *Turner Joy* patrolled in support of new South Vietnamese raids on the coast, Herrick intercepted North Vietnamese messages that gave him 'the impression' that enemy patrol boats were planning another attack. The captain requested carrier aid and eight Crusader jets were soon overhead. About ten o'clock, urgent calls came from both ships' sonar operators: scopes showed a number of enemy torpedoes coming in. The ships erupted into action, taking evasive maneuvers while firing wildly into the night.

When the shooting died down after two hours, 22 incoming torpedoes had been counted and US officers claimed 2 or 3 kills on enemy craft. But Captain Herrick was not so sure. None of the supposed enemy torpedoes had struck the US ships, and not one enemy vessel had been spotted either visually or on sonar. After quizzing his sonar operators, he reported to Admiral Sharp that the screen blips probably showed 'freak weather effects,' not torpedoes. In short, the US destroyers might have been firing at phantoms.

President Johnson was not interested in such uncertainties.

Previous pages: *General William C Westmoreland inspects three combat-ready Hawk anti-aircraft missiles at Danang Airbase: 21 February 1965.*

Below: *A supply ship comes alongside the aircraft carrier USS Oriskany during operations in the Gulf of Tonkin.*

Far left: *A US Navy A-1H Skyraider returns to the USS* Kitty Hawk *after a mission. The plane carries up to 8000 pounds of ordnance.*

Left: *An American pilot captured after his plane was shot down over North Vietnam was photographed by the Hanoi government as evidence of their success against US air raids. It was claimed that five other planes had been downed at the same time.*

Right: *A US Navy A-4 Skyhawk, manufactured by McDonnell Douglas. This light attack aircraft has a range of 700 miles and was used throughout the Vietnam War.*

Left: *A Skyhawk based on the USS* Oriskany *releases its load of 500-lb bombs.*

Right: *The USS* Bennington *off the coast of Vietnam.*

This time he ordered reprisal air strikes, chosen from lists prepared in May and given the codename 'Pierce Arrow.' As the planes headed for their Northern targets, the president made a television broadcast in which he claimed that the strikes were in response to two 'unprovoked' attacks on American ships. He did not mention the uncertainties surrounding the second attack, or the fact that the ships were spying. He assured the world, 'We still seek no wider war.'

On 5 August, American fighter-bombers from the *Constellation* and *Ticonderoga* flew 64 sorties over a 100-mile area of the North Vietnamese coast on the Gulf of Tonkin, destroying a number of PT boats, an oil storage depot, and anti-aircraft installations. Two planes were downed and pilot Everett Alvarez, Jr, parachuted into the North, not to emerge from prison until 1973. The air strikes brought the usual condemnation from communist nations, but American allies were generally supportive.

The Tonkin Gulf Resolution, drafted by William Bundy

months earlier for just such a contingency, passed the House and Senate on 7 August, empowering the president to 'take all necessary measures to repel any armed attack against the forces of the United States and to prevent further aggression . . . including the use of armed force, to assist any member . . . of the Southeast Asia Collective Defense Treaty.' There were only two dissenting votes in Congress: Senators Wayne Morse and Ernest Gruening suspected the truth, despite flat denials from Secretary McNamara that US ships in the Gulf had been supporting South Vietnamese raids. In any case, Johnson now had all the authority he needed to put into motion the elaborate plans made by the military during recent months.

Although there was pressure from Admiral Sharp to 'confirm absolutely' the second Gulf attack, Captain Herrick was never convinced. Later studies have concluded that it almost certainly never happened. President Johnson himself privately opined of the incident that took America over the brink into war, 'Hell, those dumb stupid sailors were just shooting at flying fish.'

New Turmoil in South Vietnam

After General Nguyen Khanh, an ARVN corps commander, overthrew Big Minh's ineffective military junta in January 1964, the social and political deterioration of South Vietnam continued apace. General Maxwell Taylor arrived in July to take over the ambassadorship from Henry Cabot Lodge; to his dismay, Taylor found Khanh and Air Force general Nguyen Cao Ky calling loudly for US support of outright attacks on the North. At the same time, Saigon was falling into anarchy and the corrupt Khanh government could do nothing to stop it. Once again, an American ambassador was expected to prop up an unworkable regime.

The most volatile issue continued to be the power struggle between Buddhists and Catholics, the former accusing the Khanh government of carrying on Diem's 'anti-Buddhist' policies. In late August 1964, after street violence caused immense destruction and claimed a number of lives, Khanh made a show of resignation and left Saigon, but he retained the title of prime minister and the real power in a provisional triumvirate (which included the ubiquitous Big Minh). Taylor still viewed Khanh as the man to support, and approved when the general quickly returned to dissolve the triumvirate and proclaim himself premier (after trying to bribe two leading Buddhists to support him). Khanh weathered a coup attempt in mid-September and later in the month successfully put down, with US help, a revolt by one of the *montagnard* tribes. The

mountain men had started hostilities by slaughtering 50 ARVN troops at a US Special Forces Camp (the ARVN and the US Green Berets were training the tribesmen in guerrilla fighting).

However, Khanh was never able to establish his power decisively, so the surrealistic political situation continued: Khanh resigned in October, but in December he and Ky engineered yet another coup. At that point, an exasperated Taylor called Khanh and his henchmen together and gave them a tongue-lashing worthy of a high-school coach: 'I told you all clearly . . . we Americans were tired of coups. Apparently I wasted my words. Now you have made a real mess. We cannot carry you forever if you do things like this.' Predictably, Khanh then took to the radio to denounce Taylor and accuse the United States of 'colonialism.'

The result was deadlock in US-South Vietnamese relations while Buddhists rampaged – and immolated themselves –- in the streets again. In late January 1965, the Armed Forces council overthrew another attempt at a civilian government and re-installed Khanh as strongman; a month later, dissident troops moved in and Khanh fled. His right arm, General Ky, finally agreed that Khanh must go; the general was appointed a 'roving ambassador.' For a few months thereafter, a civilian government ruled uneasily. General Westmoreland asked Washington for two battalions of US Marines to help stabilize the worsening military situation.

Above: *Montagnard tribesmen pass in review during a 1965 parade in Saigon to commemorate the overthrow of the Diem regime two years before.*

Far left: *Gifts of food and clothing from the United States are distributed by a US Army officer at district headquarters in Ben Cat.*

Left: *ARVN soldiers with dogs guard a group of Vietnamese villagers during a search for suspected Vietcong.*

Vietnam in US Politics

As the 1964 presidential campaign heated up, Johnson's Great Society program promised to climax a historic decade of liberal pathbreaking in the areas of civil rights and the reduction of poverty. The president's greatest fear (which was to be realized) was that war in Vietnam would set back the social programs that were so close to his heart. His commitment to Vietnam, however, so far as the public understood it, also enjoyed general approval.

To defeat Republican challenger Barry Goldwater, who was considerably more conservative than the national mood, Johnson simply had to avoid making any sudden and inauspicious moves – such as starting a full-scale war. As mentioned earlier, the president's tactic was to paint Goldwater as a warmonger and himself as the moderate. Goldwater leaped into that trap in May, when he proposed using low-yield atomic bombs to strike supply lines from China to North Vietnam. Public alarm soon forced Goldwater to backtrack on that idea, but his gaffe sharpened the image of a moderate, sagacious Johnson.

The essence of Republican criticism of the president was not that he was preparing to fight a war – Goldwater proclaimed that 'extremism in the defense of liberty is no vice' – but that he *was* fighting a war without telling the American people about it. Moreover, he was not fighting it vigorously enough. Goldwater was reduced to charging that US servicemen were dying in Viet-

nam because they were flying obsolescent planes, which implied that he would give them better planes.

In June 1964, Henry Cabot Lodge resigned as ambassador to South Vietnam to make a stab at the Republican presidential nomination. In August, after Goldwater had secured the nomination, Johnson sent Lodge to Europe to sell America's Vietnam involvement to its allies. Lodge secured pledges of technical support from several countries and general agreement that the war was a 'free world' issue rather than a simple civil war. France, which had long called for a recognition of neutrality for its old colony, did not join in the chorus of support. In the end, however, no Western European country would contribute military aid to the war.

As the election drew near, Johnson had convinced the country that he was a man of peace, though ever vigilant against communism. In August he said that the nation had 'tried very carefully to restrain ourselves and not to enlarge the war.' The United States, he said, would continue to aid the South Vietnamese but would not fight a war for them; Goldwater repeatedly challenged Johnson to admit he was on the verge of doing just that. Leading comfortably in the polls, Johnson had no need to respond. In November 1964, he regained the presidency by a landslide. The war in Vietnam was becoming the paramount issue in US politics.

Above: *A peace-oriented commercial for Johnson in the 1964 election campaign.*

Left: *The magnitude of Johnson's victory was due in part to public belief that he was the candidate least likely to escalate US involvement in Vietnam.*

Right: *A hut abandoned by the Vietcong during an attack by the Vietnamese 8th Airborne Battalion. Food was still cooking over the fire when the South Vietnamese soldiers entered the area.*

The Covert War Continues

By 1964 the Ho Chi Minh Trail, extending through Laos near the Vietnamese border, had become an efficient route, moving communist infiltrators plus tons of weapons, supplies, and food, from the North to the South. Tens of thousands of laborers, equipped with the latest Soviet and Chinese equipment, worked daily to improve the trail and to repair it after air strikes. These workers were backed up by their own barracks, workshops, warehouses, hospitals, and anti-aircraft defenses. All in all, it was a testament to the remarkable sophistication of Hanoi's logistics: carrying supplies on their backs and on bicycles as much as on trucks, the communists were able to supply a full-scale war in the South despite everything the United States could throw at the Ho Chi Minh Trail.

US Navy and Air Force jets began to make low-altitude reconnaissance flights over Laos in May 1964, under the codename 'Yankee Team.' Laotian leader Souvanna Phouma secretly approved the flights, while maintaining his facade of neutrality. Within a month, two Yankee Team planes were downed by the communist Pathet Lao, and Washington ordered armed jets to accompany the observation planes and to attack the Pathet Lao on the ground. Through years of escalating covert air war in Laos, the United States would claim publicly that it was only pursuing 'reconnaissance flights.' In October 1964, Laos secretly entered the Vietnam War. After much pressure from the United States, Laotian Air Force jets began bombing North Vietnamese and Vietcong infiltration routes, with US fighters accompanying them to keep away Soviet-made MiGs.

By early December 1964, President Johnson had received a popular mandate in the election and was ready to begin, tentatively, to escalate the air war enough to damage the communists, but not enough to risk the very real and sobering threat of direct Soviet and/or Chinese intervention. Johnson and his advisors approved a two-phase bombing plan. Phase I, under the name 'Operation Barrel Roll,' was the successor of Yankee Team; it ordered a secret bombing campaign against communist positions along the Ho Chi Minh Trail in southern Laos, carried out by planes from carriers stationed in the South China Sea. (Phase II of the new air war, as described later, involved

'Rolling Thunder' air strikes on North Vietnam.) Beginning in mid-December 1964, Barrel Roll would go on, in secret, for nearly a decade. 'Operation Steel Tiger,' begun in Laos in 1965, mounted massive strikes on the trail itself. During all this time, despite the countless tons of bombs, napalm, and defoliants expended, enemy traffic along the trail would increase steadily.

For years the United States had carried on covert DeSoto Missions off the coasts of China, Russia, and North Korea. US ships monitored signals from communist shore installations, mapped coasts, and kept track of seagoing traffic. It was such a DeSoto operation, in support of South Vietnamese commando and PT-boat raids on the North Vietnamese coast, that led to the Gulf of Tonkin incident. The DeSoto missions would continue for years to come, as the US Navy played an increasing part in the war. All classes of warship served in Vietnam, from nuclear carriers to river craft.

Above: *A US Air Force F-100 Super Sabre fires a pod of folding-fin rockets. This plane was widely used for escort duty, including flak suppression missions.*

Top: *A US Air Force bomber strikes a Vietcong position in the jungle of South Vietnam during 1965, the year of the major US buildup.*

Above: *Early Operation Barrel Roll missions were carried out by Navy A-5 Vigilantes like these, accompanied by F-4B Phantoms and RF-8A photo-reconnaissance aircraft.*

At the beginning of 1965, the United States had about 23,000 personnel in South Vietnam and had lost 140 killed and 1138 wounded during the previous year. The South's ARVN forces numbered some 265,000, roughly divided between paramilitary and militia units. In support of the American effort, South Korea had sent some 2000 advisors, and there were small units from Australia and New Zealand. Thailand and the Philippines were readying units to send in. On the other side, a continuous stream of Southern-born, North Vietnamese-trained National Liberation Front fighters, the Vietcong, were moving south; by the beginning of 1965 they numbered some 34,000, with another 80,000 active sympathizers in South Vietnam. In addition, by 1965 North Vietnamese Army (NVA) units were beginning to move into the South. Responding to the situation, America was about to end its reliance on covert operations to help South Vietnam fight the war: the year 1964 would prove to be the last in which US troops were designated 'military advisors' to the South Vietnamese.

Above: *North Vietnamese troops man a 37mm anti-aircraft gun against US warplanes during the stepped-up air raids of 1965.*

Right: *A member of the Vietnam Junk Force searches a local fishing vessel for Vietcong infiltrators or supplies.*

Above: *US Air Force F-105 Thunderchiefs release 1000-lb bombs over a communist barracks 30 miles northeast of Dien Bien Phu – October 1965.*

Left: *A member of the 1st Air Cavalry Division stands watch while fellow soldiers unload supplies from a giant C-130 transport.*

Vietnam on the International Stage

As American commitment to the fighting in Vietnam, and Vietcong response to it, escalated in tandem, the nations of the world began to make known their loyalties and policies. Soon after the Gulf of Tonkin incident, Hanoi rejected a United Nations call for Security Council debate on the conflict, saying that it was a matter for signatories of the Geneva Accords. Thereafter, split between American and communist factions, the UN could do little but call vainly for negotiations.

Most traditional American allies officially approved the Vietnam policy, but France, having suffered its own debacle in the region, was distinctly unenthusiastic about the new situation and called for negotiations and recognition of Vietnamese neutrality. Britain, while nominally supporting American actions, politely kept its distance. A few countries – South Korea, Australia, New Zealand, and Canada – would send troops into action, but never in large numbers. Although it was theoretically a Western struggle for democracy and freedom, the war was to remain essentially an American/South Vietnamese operation.

The Soviet Union and China repeatedly threatened intervention, but neither country made any real preparations for military involvement. Their material support of North Vietnam, while essential to the communist war effort, was to prove chronically stingy. (Later in the war, a North Vietnamese joke ran: 'NLF to Russia: Send more supplies. Russia to NLF: Tighten your belts. NLF to Russia: Send belts.') From Cuba, Fidel Castro dispatched advisors to train the Vietcong in guerrilla tactics.

Japan was cool to the whole affair; Prime Minister Sato told the National Press Club in Washington that Vietnam should be a matter for Asians. In April 1965, 17 nonaligned nations called for 'a peaceful solution through negotiations'; similar calls were voiced by everyone from African nations to the pope, but to no avail. President Johnson said that peace was contingent on the cessation of Vietcong aggression. North Vietnam, which had been the loser more than once in negotiations, had concluded that only fighting would make a difference now. The communists distrusted the United States completely and had little confidence in the good will of other nations.

Top right: *An Australian Armour Regiment's tank commanders are briefed on their newly arrived 50-ton British Centurion tanks at the port of Vung Tau.*

Far right: *The Republic of Korea sent troops, seen here, and money to support the South Vietnamese against the communists.*

Right: *Korean Marines pull a young woman free of a cave-in.*

The Fighting Heats Up

In the wake of the Gulf of Tonkin Resolution, the Vietcong were quick to make a show of strength to the United States. During the last days of October 1964, VC surrounded the American air base at Bienhoa, 12 miles north of Saigon. Local peasants, certainly aware of the communist presence, made no effort to alert the unsuspecting Americans. On the night of 1 November, the enemy unleashed a withering mortar attack that killed 5 US servicemen and wounded 76; 6 B-57 bombers were destroyed on the ground and a number of other aircraft damaged before the Vietcong disappeared into the jungle.

In Washington, with the election imminent, President Johnson decided not to mount retaliatory raids for the Bienhoa

Above: *South Vietnamese troops make their way across an improvised bridge.*

Top right: *An Armored Personnel Carrier (APC) disgorges men of the 1st Infantry Division north of Saigon.*

Right: *US artillerymen operate a 155mm towed howitzer.*

Left: *Bunkers constructed near Bien Hoa by the 1st Infantry Division – 1965.*

attack. This emboldened the communists to try a more impressive show of force – a co-ordinated operation in Phuoc Ty Province, some 40 miles from Saigon. With their usual efficiency, some 1000 VC troops infiltrated the area. On 28 December 1964, after small attacks around the province, they occupied the village of Binh Gia for eight hours, withdrawing only after three ARVN battalions arrived by helicopter. But the communists were not finished; on 2 January 1965, they savaged two tank-

Above: *Men of the 1st Cavalry drag a guerrilla from a bunker during a sweep north of Bong Son.*

Right: *Frightened villagers flee toward a waiting helicopter for evacuation, as Vietcong infiltrate their area.*

equipped companies of ARVN Rangers at a rubber plantation near Binh Gia. In the fighting the VC killed some 200, including 5 Americans, and wounded 300. Another surprise attack added to the casualty list on 4 January. This disastrous week moved one US officer to wonder 'how [Vietcong] troops, a thousand or more of them, could wander around the countryside so close to Saigon without being discovered. That tells something about this war.'

What told something further about the war was the fact that the South Vietnamese capital was not safe either. On Christmas Eve 1964, a pair of VC terrorists planted a bomb in Saigon's Brinks Hotel, where a number of US advisors were in residence. The blast killed 2 Americans and wounded 58. With obvious success, the Vietcong were trying to prove that they could strike at will, anytime, anyplace. And Americans were beginning to learn the despair of fighting a war in which friend and enemy looked exactly alike.

Attack at Pleiku

The next American installation to feel the sting of Vietcong operations was a helicopter base at Camp Halloway, near Pleiku in the Central Highlands. Military advisors were sleeping in their fortified compound on the morning of 7 February 1965 when Vietcong infiltrators slipped into the perimeter and opened fire; at the same time, a rain of mortar shells descended. When the fire and chaos died down and the enemy had disappeared, 8 Americans lay dead and 126 wounded; 9 helicopters and a transport plane had also been destroyed. Few enemy casualties were found; one VC killed in the perimeter had on him a detailed map of the compound.

This attack coincided with a flurry of diplomatic activity on both sides. McGeorge Bundy, President Johnson's national security advisor, was conferring with South Vietnamese leaders in Saigon. At the same time, Soviet Premier Aleksei Kosygin was in Hanoi for talks. Speculation was rife that the respective governments were being pressed to negotiate, but events of the next few days made agreements unlikely. A Soviet participant in the Hanoi talks described his North Vietnamese allies as 'a bunch of stubborn bastards.'

Upon learning of the Pleiku raid, Bundy phoned the president from Saigon to urge retaliatory air raids. Johnson convened a group of advisors, most of whom approved the idea; dissenting were Senator Mike Mansfield, soon to become a major opponent of the war, and Vice-President Hubert Humphrey, whose demurral was viewed as disloyalty by the president. A grim Johnson ordered the raids, to show the North Vietnamese that they could not strike US bases without calling down wrath from the skies.

The first retaliatory strike took to the air the same day. Under the codename Operation Flaming Dart, 49 carrier-based Navy Skyhawks and F-8 Crusaders hit guerrilla military barracks and staging areas at Donghoi, 40 miles into North Vietnam. Next day Air Vice-Marshal Nguyen Cao Ky led South Vietnamese planes in a raid on a military communications center at Vinhlinh in North Vietnam. However, the Flaming Dart raids only re-

Right: *Nguyen Cao Ky, commander of the Vietnamese Air Force, aboard the USS* Independence. *A colorful figure throughout the era of US involvement, Ky would become prime minister and vice-president of South Vietnam, but he never grasped the full power that he sought. He had to flee the country when the communists took over in 1975.*

Top: *The engine of an F-8 Crusader flames out on approach to the carrier USS* Coral Sea.

Above: *The pilot ejects from the stricken plane, to be rescued from the water some 80 seconds after immersion.*

Top right: *An F-8 Crusader on the point of recovery aboard the carrier USS* Bon Homme Richard.

Right: *Naval aircraft played a major role in the war because of their quick-response capability. The Seventh Fleet's carrier task force (TF77) operated a mix of strike, interdiction and reconnaissance planes.*

Below: *South Vietnamese laborers clear brush for a helipad to be used by the 1st Air Cavalry Division.*

inforced Hanoi's determination not to negotiate, and the Soviets agreed to step up support, providing surface-to-air missiles to the North.

International response to the raids was the usual chorus of condemnation and saber-rattling from the communist side – including 'spontaneous' civilian attacks on US embassies in Moscow and Budapest – and support from Britain and Australia. France continued to call for negotiations. In any event, Flaming Dart had no dampening effect on the VC: on 10 February they blew up the US barracks at Quinhon, killing 23 American soldiers.

Above: *North Vietnamese militiawomen return to work after a US air raid.*

Right: *Hanoi petroleum storage facility after heavy bombing by the US Air Force in 1966.*

Operation Rolling Thunder

Flaming Dart, like previous United States air strikes, had been carefully represented as a reprisal for a specific communist act of aggression. But in February 1965, with most of the American public backing his Vietnam policy, the president decided to follow the 'hawks' among his advisors and order the systematic bombing of North Vietnam. Thus began Operation Rolling Thunder, designed to bolster South Vietnamese morale, punish the North Vietnamese for their aggressions, and impede the flow of communist supplies.

The plans had long been in place, but there remained the problem of how to sell this new air war to the public. McGeorge Bundy found the right formula in the phrase 'sustained reprisal': the ongoing raids were to be presented as a general response to the North Vietnamese 'pattern of aggression.' The North, in short, was to be bombed to even the balance for all Vietcong activities in the South.

The first raid was scheduled for 20 February, but was postponed due to upheavals in the South Vietnamese government – the final fall of General Khanh. Rolling Thunder finally got underway on 2 March 1965, when over 100 US Air Force jet bombers hit an ammunition depot at Xombang, 10 miles above the 17th parallel in the North; 4 of these US planes did not come back. Meanwhile, South Vietnamese pilots bombed a naval base at Quangkhe.

Originally, the raids were intended to go on for eight weeks. In fact, they lasted for three years, with intermittent halts in hopes of negotiations. Beginning in May 1965, the second phase of Rolling Thunder would drop a daily average of 800 tons of bombs, rockets, and missiles on North Vietnam (which is about the size of Texas). The incendiary weapons called napalm were a prominent feature of the raids, as were 'Lazy Dog' antipersonnel bombs, which hurled tiny steel darts over a wide area. The targets – military installations, bridges, roads, rail lines, fuel

Top: *F-105F Thunderchiefs.*

Above: *A US Air Force A-1E Skyraider descends for a strafing run.*

Top right: *US Air Force F-100 Super Sabre.*

Right: *The RF-4C version of the Phantom, used for tactical reconnaissance.*

depots – were spread over most of the North, with forbidden zones around Hanoi, Haiphong, and the Chinese border.

Every target was chosen by President Johnson himself and his advisors from a list supplied by the Joint Chiefs of Staff. A strange spectacle began: business-suited government officials huddled over maps during Tuesday lunch in a White House dining room, debating which towns and military installations in distant North Vietnam would receive that week's rain of steel and fire. Johnson seemed to be delighted at this business of

waging war from the comfort of his own home. 'They can't even bomb an outhouse without my approval,' he boasted.

Eight-engined B-52 Stratofortress bombers, as big as a football field, were the heavies of the American air arsenal. The major B-52 operation, called Arc Light, began in June 1965. In these raids, the bombers flew from Guam to strike Vietcong concentrations in the South. Over the years, these gargantuan planes and their weapons would transform much of Vietnam into something resembling a lunar landscape.

Left: *Attack on the Thanh Hoa Bridge by Skyhawks based on USS* Oriskany, *November 1967.*

Below left: *AH-1G Cobra on a search-and-destroy mission in Tan An Province.*

Right: *An HH-3E 'Jolly Green Giant' rescue helicopter escorted by two* Sandy A-1s.

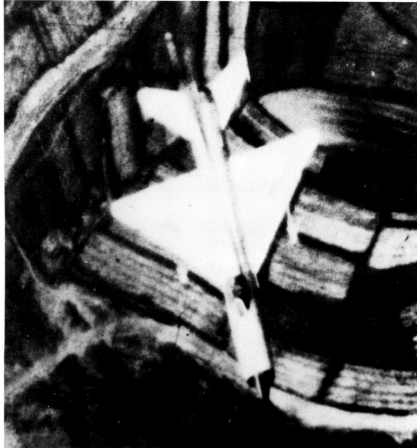

Left: *UH-1Ds return to base after landing members of the 1st ARVN Division in the A Shau Valley.*

Above: *A Russian-built MiG-21 Fishbed, photographed over Hanoi. The plane was introduced into the theater in 1966.*

The real purpose of the air war was not simply retaliation. Rather it was to cripple enemy supply lines and destroy the morale of the communists. Neither goal was achieved: the enemy war effort grew steadily throughout the years of Rolling Thunder. In 1967 Secretary of Defense Robert McNamara, who had created the air war, confessed his disillusionment: 'enemy operations in the south cannot . . . be stopped by air bombardment – short, that is, of the virtual annihilation of North Vietnam and its people.' And the United States was not quite willing to go so far as some military voices advised and 'bomb North Vietnam back into the Stone Age.' Attempts – by no means always successful – were made to avoid civilian centers in the cities and the critical dikes along the Red River, whose destruction would have drowned countless people; the latter were never destroyed. It is arguable that much of the confidence shown by the North Vietnamese came from their conviction that America would never cross the line into a campaign of total annihilation. It is arguable, as well, that such a campaign was the only way to win the war.

Top left: *During early Rolling Thunder operations, USAF bombers and strike planes such as this F-100 had to be accompanied by planes of the VNAF. Later, this requirement was dropped.*

Above: *A Strategic Air Command B-52F releases its deadly load of 750-lb bombs during Operation Arc Light – 1965. This plane was based at Andersen AFB on Guam.*

Far left: *The powerful B-52D was equipped with wing fuel tanks. Many of these bombers were based in Thailand rather than Guam on account of the shorter distance to targets in Vietnam.*

Left: *One of the F-4B Phantom 2s based on the USS* Midway.

The Marines Go In

The changeover to a sustained air war had been one critical turning point. The second turning point, commitment of American fighting troops on the ground to supersede the 'advisors,' came in March 1965. MACV commander General William Westmoreland had requested that two battalions of Marines be sent over to erect a security ring around Danang Air Base, on the coast. Over the objections of the ambassador to South Vietnam, Maxwell Taylor, Johnson agreed to the request, but did not inform the South Vietnamese government until the last minute. Piqued at this discourtesy, Chief of Staff Nuyen Van Thieu asked that the Marine landing be 'inconspicuous.' Westmoreland also wanted a low-profile landing.

The 3500 Marines who arrived between 8 and 12 March were scarcely inconspicuous, as they lumbered off landing craft in full combat gear, to be greeted by a big sign reading 'Welcome Gallant Marines,' plus TV cameras and smiling Vietnamese women who bedecked the men with garlands of flowers. Tanks, recoilless rifles, and howitzers followed the troops. Still, the press and the international public, including the communists, paid little attention to the landing. All seemed to buy Johnson's assertion that the Marines were there for a specific and limited objective.

The Leathernecks deployed around Danang. Until then, the

Above: *A Marine platoon commander signals his men.*

Top: *The first battalions of Marines come ashore at Danang.*

Right: *A member of the first Army combat unit in Vietnam – the 173rd Airborne Brigade – which arrived in May 1965.*

base had experienced only one guerrilla attack, but the presence of the Marines seemed to draw the enemy like a magnet; the troops found themselves fighting off three guerrilla attacks on one of their first nights. By May the newly named III Marine Amphibious Force (MAF) – including two fresh battalions – were dug in not only at Danang, but at installations at Phubai and Chulai as well.

Within the administration, debate was rife concerning the ultimate purpose and direction of the war. In an April 1965 speech entitled 'Why Are We in South Vietnam?' Johnson outlined for the public his own reasons: 'We are there because we have a promise to keep . . . we have made a national pledge to help South Vietnam defend its independence. We are also there to strengthen world order [and] because there are great stakes in the balance. . . . To withdraw from one battlefield means only to prepare for the next . Our objective is the independence of South Vietnam and its freedom from attack.' Behind the scenes, however, blunter ideas were being expressed. In a March 1965

Above: *The 9th Marine Expeditionary Brigade at Danang.*

Left: *The sprawling complex at Danang, in use between 1962 and 1972, was located south of the imperial city of Hué on the Gulf of Tonkin.*

Top right: *Vietcong captured by the Marines in June 1966.*

Right: *Marines of the 2nd Battalion negotiate a rice paddy in search of suspected Vietcong.*

note, McNamara assistant J T McNaughton weighted United States aims: '70% – To avoid a humiliating United States defeat (to our reputation as a guarantor); 20% – To keep SVN . . . territory from Chinese hands; 10% – To permit the people of SVN to enjoy a better, freer way of life; ALSO – To emerge from crisis without unacceptable taint from methods used. NOT – To "help a friend."' Undersecretary of State George Ball was becoming the resident devil's advocate of the administration; he had grave doubts from the beginning and said so. In July Ball wrote to the President, 'The South Vietnamese are losing the war to the Vietcong. No one can assure you that we can beat the Vietcong, or even force them to the conference table on our terms, no matter how many hundred thousand [troops] we deploy.' Ball went on to advise that no more troops be committed, that combat be avoided, and that negotiations be sought more actively.

President Johnson was not about to follow such advice, but he was becoming impatient; no progress was apparent, and the Marines were committed to defensive operations. General Westmoreland's answer to this problem – as to all problems – was more men, so he could pursue a systematic offensive on the ground. In spring 1965, having sent in the Marines with no great political fallout, Johnson was ready to assure Westmoreland that he need 'assume no limitations on funds, equipment, or personnel.' The general requested a buildup to 17 combat battalions by summer; at a Hawaii meeting in April, administration civilian and military leaders decided to double the existing commitment, to 82,000, with Australian and South Korean troops increased to 7250. Thus on 3-12 May, the first Army combat units arrived: 3500 men of the 173rd Airborne Brigade, including the first American artillery unit to enter the war. In late June the brigade, accompanied by Aussie troops and an ARVN unit, made its first excursion – an abortive offensive into a jungle area called Vietcong Zone D. The American ground war was in business.

Conflict Spreads to the Home Front

At the beginning of 1965, many Americans had no idea that the United States had troops in Vietnam. By the middle of that year, however, it was clear to all that America was fighting there, and the implications of that fact were sinking in. A Harris poll of that time showed that 57 percent of the nation supported Johnson's actions – still a majority, but already below the level of support the president hoped for. Every American war has given rise to vigorous anti-war sentiment (the Civil War and both World Wars not excepted) but the conflict in Vietnam was to produce an unprecedented division in society, one that would have repercussions and aftershocks for decades after the war.

Public demonstrations against American involvement had begun to flare in scattered locations immediately after the Gulf of Tonkin incident. Most of those demonstrations were centered on college campuses, where years of civil rights activity had taught the methods of political action to a generation of young men and women. The civil rights movement seemed to flow unbroken into the anti-war movement, with the faces the same but the acronyms changing from SCLC and NAACP to SDS and 'Yippie.'

The events that dramatically swelled the ranks of protesters were the first commitment of fighting forces in March 1965 and, more significantly, the president's announcement in late July that military forces in Vietnam were to be nearly doubled (to 125,000). As a result, monthly draft calls would increase from 17,000 to 35,000. A majority of young men at that time viewed this with equanimity or even enthusiasm, but for a growing

minority of college students, who had grown up in peaceful and prosperous times, the prospect of being drafted to fight and die in a war they could not understand or approve of was enough to send them shouting into the streets.

At the University of Michigan, the first 'teach-in,' its name reminiscent of the civil rights 'sit-in,' was held in March 1965: classes were cancelled while some 200 faculty members convened seminars on the war. This form of protest spread to other campuses, contributing to the growth of the movement. The government fueled the fire by making it illegal to destroy a draft card; students immediately began risking arrest by burning their cards at peace rallies.

To most of the nation, the protests at first seemed an unruly outbreak by spoiled and unwashed college kids – the movement coincided with the rise of drug use and a bizarre new lifestyle among youth. The word 'hippie' (from the slang term 'hip,' meaning aware of the newest trends and attitudes) was beginning to be bandied about. But from the beginning, older and wiser voices were part of the movement as well. By autumn 1965, civil rights leader Martin Luther King Jr had turned against the war; he spoke of going outside government channels to discuss negotiations with communist leaders. King's turn was bitterly criticized, both by the press (which was still largely pro-war) and by many members of the increasingly factional civil rights movement, who felt that King was getting sidetracked onto the wrong issue. Although his was a lonely and prophetic voice among black leaders at first, King continued to speak out doggedly against the war, insisting that it was very much a civil rights and a black issue, since the black and the poor were going to be the main casualties of the fighting.

Increasingly throughout 1965, citizens marched in the streets of America and of other countries around the world: in October, co-ordinated protests were mounted in London,

Top left: *Dr Martin Luther King, Jr, civil-rights and anti-war leader, accepts the Nobel Peace Prize in Oslo in 1964.*

Bottom left: *A tense confrontation between an ROTC student and an anti-Vietnam War demonstrator on the campus of Washington University, St Louis, during a series of protests.*

Right: *Some 900 students at the University of California's Berkeley campus were locked into Sproul Hall by campus police after a day-long sit-in protesting restrictions on campus political activity: 1964.*

Bottom right: *Four student pacifists burn their draft cards at a rally in March 1966.*

Below: *Peace activist Dr Benjamin Spock, supported by anti-draft demonstrators, arrives at the Federal Courthouse in Boston to answer charges of conspiring to aid draft resistance: January 1968.*

Rome, Brussels, Copenhagen, Stockholm, and 40 American cities. On 27 November, up to 35,000 demonstrators circled the White House and listened to speeches by Benjamin Spock and Coretta Scott King. Politicians were quick to sense this seismic rumble in the body politic; for some, it reinforced their own doubts, although in 1965 it was still politically risky to come out unequivocally against the war. By the end of the year, Congressional doubters had begun to make their first tentative public demurs. In December Senator Ernest Gruening declared that the conflict in Vietnam was a civil war and no threat to the United States. The same month, Representative Emmanuel Cellar criticized Selective Service director General Lewis Hershey for threatening to draft student protesters. Robert Kennedy,

who was gearing up to run for the presidency, proclaimed, 'the right to criticize and the right to dissent is in the oldest tradition of this country.' Conservative Senator Barry Goldwater labeled Kennedy's remarks 'close to treason.'

Then, during a single week in November 1965, the nation was shocked by two acts that reflected as nothing else could the depth of feeling that was growing against the war. They seemed also to show a troubling affinity of spirit with the Buddhist monks of distant, war-torn Vietnam. Two young Americans immolated themselves with gasoline in protest of the war – Quaker Norman Morrison in front of the Pentagon, Roman Catholic Roger Allen LaPorte in front of UN headquarters in New York.

The Naval War Gets Underway

The major American escalation had been triggered at sea, with the autumn 1964 Gulf of Tonkin incident (or imaginary incident) during the DeSoto Mission of destroyers *Maddox* and *Turner Joy*. The US Navy entered the shooting directly in May 1965, when warships began to shell Vietcong targets in central Vietnam. For the rest of the American involvement the Navy was to be a primary resource, with its carrier-based planes, its logistics support, and its big guns.

As the war settled in, the Seventh Fleet, some 125 ships and 64,000 men, commanded the waters off Vietnam. Its Task Force 77 included the attack carriers *Hancock*, *Coral Sea*, and *Ranger*, all carrying a mixture of strike, interdiction, and reconnaissance planes including F-8E Crusader fighters, A-4 Skyhawk fighter-bombers, and propeller-driven A-1 Skyraiders. Larger carriers like the nuclear-powered *Enterprise* carried the heavier F-4 Phantom fighters rather than the Crusaders. At the

Above: *Rockets from Navy aircraft based on the USS* Ranger *explode on their targets in the summer of 1966.*

Right: *A Navy SP-2 Neptune overflies a junk to check for the presence of supplies destined for the Vietcong.*

Left: *Suspects apprehended in a Market Time operation are transported from their junk to the radar picket escort USS* Forster *in the South China Sea. They will be transferred to Vietnamese authorities at the port of Vung Tao for questioning.*

Above: *Helicopters based on the USS* Valley Forge *descend toward a landing base, guided by signals from a Marine on the ground. Carrier-based choppers were used mainly for rescue, observation, and transport missions. The helicopter proved its value during the Korean conflict of the early 1950s and came into its own in Vietnam.*

end of 1964, TF77 arrived at 'Yankee Station,' a standing rendezvous position 75 miles offshore in the Gulf of Tonkin. From there the Flaming Dart air strikes were launched in retaliation for the Vietcong attack on Pleiku. A similar fleet was maintained at 'Dixie Station' to pursue operations in South Vietnam.

A primary task of the Navy was to enforce a blockade of the Vietnamese coast. The limitations of the American war effort, in which a gigantic military machine was brought to bear on a small country primitively supplied with materiel, can be seen in the dilemmas of Operation Market Time, in which Navy radar ships, armed 'Swift' patrol craft, various heavier vessels, and surveillance planes monitored the traffic aboard junks. The problem was that there were thousands of junks plying the coasts and rivers every week, like a swarm of insects. Most of them contained peasants innocently going about their business: some carried arms and supplies for the enemy. There was simply no way to monitor the traffic adequately when each small boat had to be laboriously stopped, boarded, and searched. Market Time did succeed in disrupting North Vietnamese supply operations on the water, but inevitably a great many supplies got through. Throughout the conflict, the enemy wore down the massive American war machine by this kind of ceaseless, antlike activity.

The job of shelling VC positions from offshore, beginning in May 1965, was handled by smaller Seventh Fleet destroyers. It soon became clear that their one or two 5-inch guns could not throw heavy shells far enough inland to damage the network of strongly reinforced bunkers the Vietcong had constructed; thus in 1967, the Navy brought up heavy cruisers like the *Newport News*, with its nine 8-inch guns, and the offshore shelling became considerably more effective. By then, however, enemy operations were on a much larger scale, and neither the shelling nor anything else seemed capable of slowing them down.

Top right: *An SP-5M Marlin seaplane searches the South Vietnamese coast for boats or junks that might be concealed in the thick vegetation that extends all the way to the waterline.*

Right: *A catapult officer gives the signal to launch an E-1 Tracker early warning aircraft from the flight deck of USS* Oriskany *during 1967 operations in the Gulf of Tonkin, Yankee Station.*

The Battle of the Ia Drang Valley

General Westmoreland's strategic ideas began with the indisputable fact that American and South Vietnamese aircraft dominated the skies over South Vietnam, which made it possible to maintain widely scattered outposts in the jungle. At the beginning of the war, US forces established fortified bases along the coast – at Danang, Phubai, Chulai, Quinhon, and Camranh. To provide a first line of defense, secondary 'fire support bases' ('firebases' for short) were placed at intervals around the main bases; later, the firebases would be scattered at strategic points around the South, both as defensive perimeters and as points of

departure for offensive operations. They could be reinforced and supplied by air with relative impunity. The main thrust of American efforts in 1965 was defensive; offensive operations were saved for major enemy threats. Such a threat materialized in mid-August, when the Vietcong were reportedly preparing to raid the Chulai airfield near Danang. In a pre-emptive strike called 'Operation Starlite,' General Lewis Walt's 3rd Marine Tank Battalion was brought in on helicopters, with amphibious tanks, fighter-bombers, and the guns of offshore cruisers in support. After three days of fighting both above ground and in tunnels, the Marines drove the enemy to the sea. It was the first all-American battle in Vietnam, and a demonstration of the new mobile firepower that was the main military development of

the war: the traditional front lines, with their logistical network stretching to the rear, were no longer seen. Now helicopters rushed men into any location to establish a defensive perimeter, and support and supply came in mostly from the skies.

The ancient mobile striking force of the cavalry survived in name in the Vietnam War, but now the cavalrymen rode a different kind of steed. The 11th Air Assault Division was formed in 1963 and spent two years testing techniques of helicopter-borne (or heliborne) operations. Renamed the 1st Cavalry Division (Airmobile), they became in 1965 the first stateside division to be sent to Vietnam. Now calling themselves the 1st Air Cavalry, they developed into one of the cornerstones of the war effort. Their equipment included cargo-carrying Chinook heli-

Left: *An Army radio operator gives his company the signal to move out on a Vietcong bugle captured during the battle for the Ia Drang Valley.*

Top: *A .30-caliber machine gun operated from the door of a UH-1B.*

Above: *The Army's UH-1B escort gunship provided a formidable fire-support platform with its flexible guns on hydraulic turrets.*

copters and the armed UH-1 'Huey' helicopter; the latter was the basic fighting and transport helicopter, its sleek profile the most familiar image of the war.

The Air Cav got its baptism of fire, and its first experience of the North Vietnamese Army, in the Battle of the Ia Drang Valley. The warmup for that battle came on 19–27 October 1965, when a contingent of North Vietnamese regulars attacked a Special Forces camp at Pleime in the Central Highlands. There 400 *montagnards*, 12 Green Berets, and South Vietnamese guerrillas repelled the attack with the help of ARVN reinforcements and allied air strikes. The enemy lost heavily. The Air Cav flew troops in and out of Pleime from its position in the heavy jungle of the Ia Drang Valley, which was known to be an enemy staging area. In fact, General Chu Huy Man was readying his North Vietnamese Army forces in the Valley for a drive southward toward

the low-lying coastal plains, which were heavily populated.

General Westmoreland ordered Major General Harry W O Kinnard, the 1st Air Cavalry commander, to 'find, fix, and defeat the enemy forces that had threatened Pleime.' Between 23 October and 20 November, Kinnard's Air Cav fought it out with General Man's forces. The 1st Squadron, 9th Cavalry, led the attack: they scouted for three days, then ran into an NVA concentration guarding a hospital and attacked them as reinforcements came up. In the first full-scale engagement of US and NVA troops in the war, the enemy was driven away. On November 3 the 1st 9th Cavalry mounted a successful VC-style ambush on NVA troops, but then found themselves under assault by an enemy battalion and had to be reinforced. After a night of fighting, the NVA pulled back.

The NVA's General Man had now lost the better part of a regi-

Left: Infantrymen board a UH-1D for return to base.

Below left: *Marines of K Company, 3rd Battalion, 1st Regiment check out a hut in Quang Tri Province during Operation Badger Tooth.*

Below: *The CH-47 Chinook could transport troops or freight.*

Above: *From mid-1965, the troop-lift role was carried out by the Army's UH-1D helicopter.*

Top right: *An encampment of the Army's 11th Cavalry Division (Airmobile).*

Center right: *Troops of G Company make their way along the fringe of the Demilitarized Zone (DMZ).*

Bottom right: *Camouflaging for a search-and-destroy mission.*

Left: *A CH-47A Chinook disgorges troops for Operation Masher, 1966.*

ment, but he was not ready to give up. He called in reinforcements, organized three regiments, and returned to the offensive. On 14 November these units began attacking Americans at Landing Zone (LZ) X-Ray; not until after a day of sustained fighting, some of it hand-to-hand, did air and artillery strikes repel the enemy. By the 16th, General Man had lost over a thousand men at LZ X-Ray. The next day, however, fighting flared again at LZ Albany, where the NVA 66th Regiment ambushed the 2nd Squadron, 7th Cavalry, killing or wounding most of Companies C and D in the first few minutes. When the enemy withdrew next morning, the column of 500 US troops had lost 150 killed and a great many seriously wounded. Sporadic fighting went on in the Ia Drang Valley for the next 10 days.

. During these weeks of fighting, American commanders refined the techniques or airborne assault that would dominate the coming years. For their part, the communists had learned that the best way to deal with American air and artillery power was to fight close: 'Grab the enemy's belt and hang on,' ran the tactical proverb.

After this battle, Westmoreland detailed the Marine 1 Corps to operate in the northern provinces of South Vietnam, the Army II Corps in the central region, the Army III Corps around Saigon, and the ARVN alone in the Mekong Delta. These deployments would prevail for some time, as the Americans settled into the war. A one-year rotation policy would apply for the duration.

Right: *A wounded Vietcong is questioned before being taken to a hospital at Lai Khe during Operation Cedar Falls.*

Below right: *'Dusters' (tank bodies converted to deliver 40mm cannon fire) move along a jungle trail.*

Below: *An 11th Cavalry tank struggles up a hill during Phase II of Operation Junction City.*

Operations 1966 – Early 1967

In Vietnam, MACV Commander Westmoreland confronted the problem that has been the despair of the generals of great armies throughout history: how to contain the wide-ranging hit-and-run tactics of a guerrilla enemy? To that end, he and his advisors evolved a ground-war strategy they were convinced would fit the fighting and the jungle terrain: a mobile, flexible defense built on the helicopter. As described, fortified firebases were established and supplied largely by air, the circular defensive perimeter replacing the old front line. Strategists spoke grandly of 'nonlinear' and 'multidirectional' combat.

The basic everyday mission was the 'search and destroy': a unit from platoon to company size would be dispatched, usually by helicopter, to sweep guerrilla-style through an area, dislodge the enemy, and 'pacify' the civilian population – which generally meant putting the fear of God into civilians and sometimes meant burning down their villages. For the men engaged in search and destroy, it was a miserable and nerve-wracking business; in contrast to the intermittent pitched battles of wars past, Vietnam troops were prey at any moment to ambush and to a host of boobytraps and mines rigged by a resourceful enemy (who made a regular cottage industry of turning unex-

ploded American bombs into highly lethal mines). Besides the enemy, there were the scourges of malaria, insects, and the dense, hot jungle. And always there were the peasants – some of them friendly, some sympathetic to the communists, some actively hostile, but all of them looking much alike and seeing American soldiers as intruders in their country.

Larger missions, carried on by a battalion or more, were called 'reconnaissance in force'; they were attempts to strike concentrations of communists and engage them in a full-scale battle. General Giap and his staff eventually learned to avoid such battles. They could not survive massive American firepower in a stand-up fight. But increasingly through 1968, Westmoreland favored these relatively cumbersome, traditional large-unit campaigns, moving with armored support through the jungle in hopes of finding a battle.

The year 1966 began with an operation called Masher/White Wing/Thang Phong II, carried out by the 1st Air Cavalry, ARVN troops, and Korean forces. The units swept through Binhdinh Province to link up with a Marine offensive called Double Eagle, which had been fighting an NVA division in the north. Masher accounted for 2389 reported enemy casualties by the

time it wound up in March. From May to July, ARVN and Army units pursued Operation Paul Revere/Than Phong 14 in Pleiku Province, claiming 546 enemy dead. In July-August 1966, 8500 Marines and 2500 ARVN mounted Operation Hastings in Quangtri Province. The target was the NVA 3224-B Division, some 10,000 strong, who had been preparing to wipe out the South Vietnamese First Infantry Division in the area. After taking an estimated 824 casualties, the enemy pulled out of the province.

Encouraged by the results of these operations, Westmoreland decided in 1967 to concentrate on large offensive efforts supported by heavy armor. The first of these, the biggest operation mounted to date in the war, was Cedar Falls, carried out in January. The objective was a Vietcong base and operations center in an area of thick jungle between Saigon and the border of Cambodia, called the Iron Triangle. The allies roared in with 16,000 US and 14,000 ARVN troops, tanks and more than 50 bulldozers.

What happened during the course of Cedar Falls demonstrates, to the hindsight of history, the limitations of what was considered a highly successful Vietnam campaign. The allies began by evicting 10,000 peasants from their homes for resettlement in 'strategic hamlets'; heavy air strikes followed over the whole area; then four villages were leveled with bulldozers to

Above: *An M-42 in action along the Cambodian border in 1967.*

Top left: *UH-1Ds evacuate troops from a battle-scarred landscape.*

Far left: *Company C troops fire upon a Vietcong bunker during Operation Masher.*

Left: *Operation White Wing helicopters move men into an assault area in February 1966.*

prevent the Vietcong political infrastructure from taking root again. Many of the enemy fled at the approach of the allies. Others were trapped in their maze of tunnels and died by the hundreds.

This juggernaut approach to war seemed to reap great rewards: besides the 711 enemy killed and 488 captured during Cedar Falls and the destruction of a major base for raids on Saigon, the United States secured mountains of Vietcong supplies and, more importantly, a half-million pages of documents detailing the entire command structure and strategic plans of both Vietcong and North Vietnamese regular army forces. Surely, here was something worth calling a major victory.

In the long run, however, Cedar Falls accomplished little. Though the Iron Triangle had been devastated, apparently beyond repair, the enemy moved right back into the area after the allied forces left. By early 1968 it was functioning smoothly as a communist operations center. The same thing was to happen time and again after the Americans withdrew from an area. As for the psychological war directed at the civilian population – few peasants who had been uprooted and seen their homes leveled by allied 'pacification' forces were encouraged to favor the South Vietnamese government. Cedar Falls and similar operations turned thousands against the American cause.

But the large-unit operations continued. Operation Lam Son 67, in February 1967, sent several battalions of the First Infantry Division to clear enemy troops from an area 13 miles south of Saigon. At the same time, the Marines' Operation Stone struck the communists south of Danang, on the coast. With these and the forthcoming Junction City campaign – indeed, throughout the years of his command – Westmoreland was pursuing a basic policy of attrition: victory was to come simply through the magnitude of enemy casualties. Progress was measured in the dismal statistics of body counts and 'kill ratios' between enemy dead and American and ARVN dead.

Such statistics, announced nightly on the evening news back in the States, were not destined to inspire support for war in the hearts and minds of the public. As the numbers mounted over the months and years, Americans grew increasingly troubled over the mountains of dead. And the notion that after a certain level of casualties the enemy would simply give up proved to be a major miscalculation: the communists had fought too long and bitterly to be discouraged by any number of dead. In ever-increasing numbers, North Vietnamese fighters set out on the long trek down the Ho Chi Minh Trail. Many of them wore armbands bearing the defiant inscription 'Born in the North, Died in the South.' General Giap had his own policy of attrition, but his had to do with time, not bodies. How long would the United States be willing to endure a stalemate before giving up? No matter how many years the Americans were in Vietnam, he reasoned, the Vietnamese Communists would be there longer.

Far left: *Members of the Vietnamese National Police and US Skytroopers of the 1st Cavalry Division make a wary inspection of village huts during a joint search operation.*

Left: *Constructing a bridge for Armored Personnel Carriers and tanks used in Junction City II, March 1967.*

Right: *A Vietcong warning discovered by members of the 5th Marines during Operation Shelby in 1967.*

Operation Junction City

In early 1967 Westmoreland trained his sights on enemy concentrations in the border areas and near the Demilitarized Zone (DMZ) between North and South Vietnam. The previous November, US forces had run afoul of Vietcong in War Zone C, a 50-by-80-kilometer area on the Cambodian border north of Saigon; a battle had developed in which the communists lost heavily. Westmoreland decided to follow up with a major operation, codenamed Junction City, in another part of War Zone C. It was to be the largest offensive of the war to date, involving 22 infantry battalions, 4 ARVN battalions, 14 artillery battalions, and tactical air support – over 25,000 men. The objective was to destroy the administrative and logistical nerve center of Hanoi's war effort in the South and to wipe out all communist forces and installations in the area.

The plan of attack was complex, but promised significant results. A mixture of infantry, airborne, ARVN, and Marine battalions were to be deployed in a horseshoe-shaped line to the north, near the Cambodian border, to block the enemy from escaping in that direction and to destroy their command center. Then the 'hammer' would strike: infantry and armored cavalry units were to attack north, smashing the enemy onto the horseshoe. After that (Phase I of Junction City), Phase II would break into separate search-and-destroy operations to mop up the area; meanwhile, the bulldozers called 'jungle eaters' would strip large tracts of land to deprive the enemy of cover.

The main thrust of Junction City was preceded by two diversionary operations during the first week of February: Operation Gadsden, along the border of Cambodia, and Operation Tucson, farther to the east. These uncovered extensive enemy supplies and installations, but met little resistance. The units of Gadsden and Tucson then moved into position in the blocking horseshoe, and Junction City itself got underway on 22 February 1967.

Other forces came in by air, one group by parachute – the first such assault since the Korean War. The hammer began to descend on 23 February, and at that point the plan that had looked so good on paper began to reveal its weaknesses. Attacking units of the hammer formation needed to be virtually shoulder-to-shoulder to prevent the enemy from slipping away, but in fact many of the units were deployed in widely spaced columns, with plenty of room for leakage in between. Besides allowing many communists to walk out, this deployment also set up ideal conditions for ambushes and flank attacks. One infantry company stumbled onto a Vietcong base camp and took blistering fire from entrenched enemy soldiers before air support arrived; the next day, the VC camp was deserted. After three days of operation, Junction City had accounted for only 42 Vietcong killed, while 14 Americans were dead and 93 were wounded. The enemy was slipping through the sieve.

Left: *A villager suspected of aiding the Vietcong is questioned by an ARVN soldier. The 'strategic hamlet' program of the early 1960s, designed to isolate South Vietnamese villagers from Vietcong infiltrators, had to be abandoned because it was so unpopular. Forcible relocation of villagers to stockades surrounded by trenches and barbed wire was widely resented.*

Below: *The CH-54 Tarhe (center) could airlift heavy equipment into the field and recover damaged helicopters for return to base.*

Left: *Members of the 173rd Airborne Battalion prepare to board a C-130 during Operation Junction City.*

Left: *US Army paratroopers line up to jump from an Air Force transport during Junction City.*

Right: *An APC damaged by a mine is repaired by members of the 11th Armored Cavalry Regiment south of Tay Ninh: February 1967.*

Within a few more days, however, concentrations of VC were located, and two battles flared near a stream called Prek Klok. The first came on 28 February, when a US infantry company was hit by enemy fire as it moved through the heavy jungle; pinned down and surrounded, the captain followed the usual procedure, calling in air and artillery support. The jets roared in and the big guns unlimbered, turning the area around the trapped company into an inferno. Enemy fire quickly died down and helicopter-borne reinforcements arrived in the afternoon. The company had lost 25 dead and 28 wounded; 167 communists were dead on the field.

The second battle near Prek Klok broke out on 10 March, when VC mounted a full-scale assault on Artillery Fire Support Base II inside the horseshoe on Route 4. The firebase contained two artillery batteries and a detachment of Army Engineers. The fighting began with an enemy mortar barrage, followed by a VC ground attack. After a full night of fighting, during which US support units mounted hundreds of air strikes and fired over 5000 artillery rounds, the VC withdrew, leaving 197 dead.

Phase I of Junction City ended on 17 March, by which time the communists had lost an estimated 835 killed and many supplies and facilities. But it was a disappointing outcome. Once again, US forces had lumbered into the jungle like a steamroller and most of the enemy had bolted like rabbits. Then began the four-week Phase II, in which smaller units pursued independent search-and-destroy missions in the area. Three times during Phase II, the enemy tried and failed to overrun American fire-bases. On the 19th of March, Fire Support Base 20 was hit by VC swarming from the jungle after the usual preliminary mortar barrage. The firebase called in one of the deadly AC-47D gunships called 'Puff the Magic Dragon' or 'Spooky'; the plane was fitted with three six-barrelled Gatling-type guns that could spray a target with 18,000 rounds per minute. Despite the Spooky, the VC pressed on and actually began climbing onto the defenders' armored personnel carriers. The perimeter was ready to break when reinforcements arrived to drive the enemy away. Communist dead totaled 227. American losses were 3 killed and 63 wounded.

Next, the enemy hit Fire Base Gold, mounting a human-wave attack in broad daylight that quickly broke into the perimeter. For over an hour, the defending artillerists frantically fired

Above: *A CH-47 lifts a disabled 'Huey' out of the battle zone during Operation Junction City.*

Right: *Infantrymen hack at vines immobilizing their tank during a push through the jungle to break a trail for lighter vehicles behind them.*

'beehive' rounds (canisters full of metal darts) and high explosive shells into masses of enemy at point-blank range before reinforcements and armor arrived to repel the VC, who had lost 647 dead. American casualties at Fire Base Gold were 15 killed, 28 wounded. The final battle of Junction City's Phase II broke out on 31 March, at Fire Support Base George. An American reconnaissance platoon was jumped near the firebase landing zone; it took reinforcements plus massive air and artillery intervention to extract the platoon and get its members back into the base. Early next morning George was hit by hundreds of mortar rounds and the enemy swarmed into the perimeter. Savage hand-to-hand fighting in darkness ensued before artillery and air strikes had slaughtered enough VC to stall their advance. An American counterattack restored the perimeter. Enemy dead at Fire Support Base George were 491, US casualties, 17 killed and 102 wounded. (Throughout the war, estimates of enemy dead were exaggerated to a greater or lesser degree, but communist losses were indeed higher than American by a ratio averaging ten to one. It was that fact as much as anything that sustained the illusion of progress.)

General Westmoreland had planned Junction City as a model operation, and he was quick to declare it a victory and the $25 million it had cost to be well spent. He dismissed General Vo Nguyen Giap's claim of a 'big victory for the Vietcong.' Exaggerated enemy body counts aside, the 'kill ratio' was immensely in the Americans' favor, and US forces had repelled the communists in five battles. But hidden beneath the impressive statistics and Westmoreland's public optimism was the fact that the bulk of the enemy had escaped the net, and US reconnaissance personnel noted that as soon as Junction City forces left, the Vietcong returned to War Zone C and went back into business as usual.

Above: *An eerie AC-119G Shadow gunship circles above Nha Trang.*

Top left: *A Marine of Delta Company on the alert.*

Top right: *Vietcong weapons captured by the US Army during operations in 1967.*

Right: *Operation MacArthur: November 1967.*

The War in the Delta

Some 90 percent of South Vietnam's travel routes lay not on roads but along the rivers. Thus, in their war, the French had pursued extensive river operations, and the Americans would be forced to follow suit. The focus of effort was the Mekong Delta, with its network of inland canals, creeks, rivers, and tidal bayous, which were plied by some 50,000 junks. Into that traffic the communists slipped their daily food and supplies: the Vietcong were fed by Mekong Delta rice.

The Navy set up the River Patrol Force in 1965. Their activities over the next 10 years would be carried on under the title Operation Game Warden – an appropriate name for the kind of deadly hide-and-seek they would be engaged in. The early workaday Game Warden vessels were the River Patrol Boats (PBRs); these 30+-foot craft were driven by waterjets, obviating the need for vulnerable propellers and rudders, and were armed with three machine guns. For a time, however, the riverine troops preferred to use leftover French armored landing craft and personnel boats of World War II vintage. Soon the Navy developed new kinds of craft better designed for this kind of warfare. The most spectacular were the 'river monitors,' built over older landing craft hulls. These ships had gun turrets resembling those of Civil War-era ironclads and were formid-

Left: A crewman mans an M-60 machine gun as his craft patrols a coastal river.

Left: *A door gunner aboard a UH-1B Iroquois helicopter surveys a Mekong Delta village.*

Center: *An Armored Troop Carrier (right) and an Assault Support Patrol Boat along a canal bank.*

Above: *Members of the Vietnamese Mobile Strike Force operate an airboat on the Mekong River.*

ably armed with a mortar, flamethrowers, Bofers and Oerlikon guns, and machine guns. Later versions added a 10-inch howitzer and bar armor. The River Patrol Craft (RPC) had twin machine guns fore and aft and a single machine gun above the conning position.

As the requirements of river fighting in Vietnam were better understood, the number of specialized craft multiplied. For command headquarters there were Command and Control Boats (CCBs). The Armored Troop Carrier (ATC) ferried soldiers, vehicles, and supplies; some also sported a steel heli-copter pad. A smaller version, the 'mini-ATC,' could race at 28 knots to land special forces on raids. These boats could carry up to 20 troops but drew only one foot of water. Giant barracks ships and barges housed forces for river operations. (The troops involved could be Navy, Army, Marine, or ARVN; as head of MACV, General Westmoreland controlled much of the river operations, which led to unprecedented Navy-Army co-oper-ation.) Later in the river war, two large Air-Cushion Vehicles (ACVs) were tried out, but they proved too delicate for the demands of the job. By late 1966 there were some 80 riverine craft in the Mekong Delta, supported by a helicopter squadron. Other riverine units patrolled widely around South Vietnam.

Top: *The marshy Mekong Delta provided innumerable hiding places for enemy craft.*

Above: *Small craft tied up to their mother ship in the Delta.*

Left: *US Navy Assault Support Patrol Boats.*

Above: *An LCPL covers a Navy Landing Craft transporting a SEAL team into enemy territory.*

Right: *A UH-1D lands on a detachable platform installed on a Navy ATC of River Assault Flotilla One.*

Among the first tasks of the river forces was to contribute to the South Vietnamese government's 1965 'Open Arms' drive, in which communist guerrillas were urged to defect with a guarantee of amnesty. The river craft helped to ferry Vietnamese Popular Force units during this program and to distribute propaganda and broadcast appeals. Open Arms had some success. Soon after, the Navy Sea, Air and Land platoons (SEALs) arrived to pursue counterinsurgency.

In February 1967 the ongoing operation was reorganized as the Riverine Assault Force. The techniques of fighting along the waterways had by then reached a high degree of sophistication: the Mobile Afloat Forces (MAFs) were stationed in floating barracks and protected by Assault Support Patrol Boats (ASPBs) and by onshore infantry and artillery. Troops were ferried into action by ATCs and helicopters, supported by monitors and ASPBs, while reserve forces waited in additional ATCs. A MAF battalion could fight in the field over a 15-square-mile area for up to 6 days with these tactics.

The war the riverine units fought was a grinding daily business, with few major battles but a constant state of alertness and an incessant threat of ambush and sabotage. Among the enemies were the heat and humidity of the swamps and the ubiquitous insects. An example of the largely unsung river search-and-destroy operations was Coronado V, which began in September 1967. The objective was to catch a VC battalion between two units, one advancing on land and the other disembarking from a flotilla on the river Rach Ba Rai.

Sailing toward the landings, the flotilla was hit by stiff VC fire from the banks; one boat got through to land its troops, but the others turned back temporarily due to heavy casualties, then tried again – only to meet the same fire from the banks. This time the boats broke through and landed the troops, who attempted to move south toward the oncoming overland unit but bogged down under heavy enemy resistance. Having defeated the American attempt at encirclement, the VC vanished overnight, and Coronado ended by default. The operation accounted for 213 enemy dead, but cost 16 Americans killed and 146 wounded.

Despite many similar frustrations, the riverine war in the Mekong Delta did reap some dividends in interdicting enemy supply lines, but it was by no means enough to change the outcome. During the 'Vietnamization' period of the Nixon administration, most of the riverine ships would be turned over to the South Vietnamese Navy, who in turn would abandon them to the victorious communists. In 1981 it would be estimated that up to 563 former American vessels were serving in Hanoi's much-expanded navy.

Chemicals at War

Left: *The 10-year defoliant-spraying program would release some 19 million gallons of herbicides – primarily Agent Orange – over Vietnam.*

Right: *Military installations along the South Vietnamese border were the target of 1967 offensives preparatory to Tet.*

Below: *Trees felled by bombing litter a landing zone.*

One of the primary allies of the communists in Vietnam was the jungle itself: the thick canopy of vegetation blanketing the countryside was an ideal cover for guerrilla activities. The response of Robert McNamara and the Defense Department to this problem was typical of their approach. If the jungle sheltered the enemy, then mobilize United States technology and power to attack it.

Bombs could do the job only to a limited extent; they created plenty of holes, but did not destroy the cover effectively. The big bulldozers called 'jungle eaters' could plow enormous swaths through the trees, but they had to be laboriously brought in and protected from attack. The simplest solution to the problem was defoliant chemicals sprayed from planes; relatively safe and easy, and highly effective – or at least it seemed so at the time.

The defoliant program was one of the first big American operations to gear up in Vietnam. In 1962, C-123 Providers began the 'Ranch Hand operation,' billed as 'modern technological area-denial' – in other words, killing the vegetation around communist supply routes and concentration areas and destroying crops suspected of supplying the enemy. Over the next 10 years, Ranch Hand planes would spray an estimated 19 million gallons of defoliating herbicides over some 20 percent of the country. In 1965 US forces also experimented with using non-toxic smoke and tear gas on Vietcong hideouts.

The favored chemical for defoliant operations was named for the color of its metal containers – Agent Orange. Besides being highly effective for the job, however, this compound contained the chemical dioxin, which is a potent carcinogen and has other still-mysterious long-range effects on those exposed to it. After the war, thousands of veterans exposed to Agent Orange began to suffer from cancer and skin diseases, and experienced birth defects in their offspring and other health problems. When these effects began showing up during the 1970s, the Defense Department at first denied that American soldiers had been exposed to Agent Orange. When that was proven to be untrue, the government began a long and so far generally successful effort to tie up the question in the courts and in scientific uncer-

tainties about the chemical's effects. However, in 1984 one group of 15,000 Vietnam veterans won an out-of-court settlement against seven chemical manufacturers in a highly publicized suit.

Agent Orange was officially banned by the Pentagon in April 1970, but soon thereafter the United States command admitted that planes had continued to use it to destroy cover and crops in Vietnam. By the time the Americans left, vast stretches of the country had been laid waste and the tons of chemicals left in the soil were a biological time bomb with unpredictable consequences for the future. Agent Orange and other defoliants will continue for generations to affect the Vietnamese population, born and unborn, far more than they affect American veterans. As for the effect of defoliant spraying upon enemy operations, despite all the United States could do, communist trucks still made their way across the devastated moonscape that their trails had become and their supplies not only got through unabated but the traffic increased.

Battle at Dakto

In the 1950s Ho Chi Minh had told the French, 'You can kill ten of my men for every one I kill of yours. But even at those odds, you will lose and I will win.' By 1967 the Americans were also accounting for about ten enemy dead for every US fatality. But the same men who had defeated the French were still directing Hanoi's war effort, and their thinking was running along the same lines.

General Vo Nguyen Giap concentrated on small-scale guerrilla operations for several months after seeing what US firepower could do in the Ia Drang Valley and the Junction City operation, but by mid-1967 he was making plans for a massive offensive during the Tet (Lunar New Year) holiday in January 1968. It was not necessarily intended to send the Americans running and end the war, although that would have been the ideal outcome. Rather, the offensive was designed to create widespread alarm and destruction and, at the very least, to demonstrate the power of combined communist forces. Offensives preparatory to the major explosion would fall on American installations along the South Vietnamese border – initially Conthien, Locninh, and the base at Dakto.

The Conthien base, five miles from the DMZ, came under daily North Vietnamese artillery fire beginning in May 1967. There, on 1 September, intensified shelling and ground attacks crashed onto the 1000 men of the 3rd Battalion, 9th Marines; this was the beginning of the long buildup to the Tet offensive. The Americans at Conthien had already been sapped by the daily barrage and by heavy rains that turned the ground into a morass of mud that gave rise to 'trenchfoot' and harbored deadly unexploded shells. As they spent day after day scrambling through the mud to escape incoming mortar rounds, the Marines began to call themselves 'the walking dead.'

The only way to break the siege was by air. In Operation Neutralize, the whole apparatus of American air, artillery, and naval firepower was brought to bear on the area with an almost unimaginable intensity. Over a seven-week period, there were 790 raids by the gigantic B-52s alone; more than 3000 other air sorties dropped some 40,000 tons of bombs in the small area around Conthien. By 4 October the enemy had withdrawn. General Westmoreland observed of Conthien that 'it was a Dien Bien Phu in reverse. The North Vietnamese lost well over 2000 men killed.' But Conthien was soon hit by artillery fire again, and similar communist operations were gearing up elsewhere.

On 27 October 1967, a North Vietnamese regiment hit an ARVN post in Songbe, the capital of Phuoc Long Province; the outnumbered ARVN repelled the enemy in heavy fighting. Two days later, Vietcong attacked a US Special Forces camp at Loc-ninh, near the Cambodian border. Soon reinforced by two infantry battalions, the Americans fought the enemy from house to house for 10 days and drove them from the town with estimated losses of over 900 killed; 50 US and South Vietnamese troops died in the battle.

The day the fighting subsided at Locninh, the enemy initiated what would develop into one of the bloodiest engagements of the war – at Dakto, near the Cambodian border north of Saigon. There the United States had established a large military complex including an airfield, ammunition dump, and South Vietnamese militia camp. A communist defector revealed to the American command that the NVA 1st Division was planning a major effort to smash the Dakto base. The 1000 US troops there were quickly reinforced by 4500 men, who prepared for the attack as air strikes began roaring overhead. The enemy, meanwhile, had been building a network of roads and bunkers around the entire area, using their rudimentary but effective tools: hands, spades, and water buffalo.

The battle began on 3 November 1967, when two American infantry companies came under NVA fire as they patrolled a ridge south of Dakto. With air and artillery support, the troops drove the enemy from the ridge. Next day, two infantry companies destroyed an enemy post and established a firebase to the southwest. The fighting escalated over the next few days, as

Left: *A member of the 1st Infantry Division sets off smoke grenades from a treetop to signal his battalion's position to jet pilots delivering air strikes nearby.*

Below left: *A US infantryman signals a frightened refugee to keep her head down during an ambush by the Vietcong.*

Right: *A rifleman cleans his weapon before going out on patrol near Chu Lai late in 1967.*

Below: *Men of the 35th Artillery, attached to the 9th Infantry, load a 155mm howitzer during Operation Coronado in the steaming Mekong Delta.*

the communists concentrated in the area and American troops constructed defenses.

On the morning of 11 November, some 200 infantrymen, Task Force Black, were on patrol near the base when a well-prepared NVA ambush erupted around them. The stricken task force frantically pulled together a defensive perimeter as the enemy completed their encirclement. With half the men wounded or killed, those still mobile kept up a furious fire at the NVA troops attacking onto the perimeter. The usual supporting air strikes were impossible due to the thick jungle. After several hours of intermittent fighting, most members of the patrol were dead or wounded, and ammunition was running low. Finally, late in the morning, reinforcements arrived by helicopter and fought their way to Task Force Black, screaming into the perimeter at a dead run. By mid-afternoon the shooting had died down. On the ground were 20 Americans killed and 154 wounded. Two were missing and only a few were untouched. The enemy body count was estimated at 75, although the soldier reporting nearly doubled the total to make US losses look less grievous, a common practice of the war. All the same, Task Force Black had mobilized its defenses to survive a vicious ambush.

A few days later, on 15 November, the NVA began 'walking' their mortar rounds systematically across Dakto, looking for the vulnerable ammunition dumps. That evening the shells found one: 'It looked like Charlie had gotten hold of some nuclear weapons,' one soldier said of the resultant explosion. By then, decimated by American sweeps in the area, the NVA were already beginning to withdraw. However, heavy fighting was required to dislodge the enemy from installations in the area: on Hill 1338, where the NVA had dug an enormous complex of bunkers; on Hill 1416, where 2 ARVN battalions fought for 4 days; and on Hill 875, where the communists held extensive fortifications to cover the retreat of the main body. On 19 November US troops moved out to assault Hill 875. It proved to be a costly business. Despite air strikes on the summit, they found themselves taking enemy fire from all directions. By nightfall, US troops were pinned down on a hill swarming with NVA soldiers who had emerged from the maze of bunkers and tunnels that honeycombed Hill 875. Then disaster fell from the sky.

A US jet, flying in the dark to strike enemy positions, released a 500-lb bomb short of the target; the bomb fell squarely into the American command post and aid station in the middle of the perimeter. Forty-two Americans died in the blast, including most of the company leaders. One survivor of the explosion recalled of that terrible night, 'You slept with the corpses. I slept under Joe. He was dead, but he kept me warm.' Over the next few days, reinforcements combined with air and artillery strikes drove the enemy from Hill 875; the fight there had been the climax of the Battle of Dakto. In 19 days of battle, the communists had lost an estimated 1455 dead; American casualties were 285 killed, 985 wounded, and 18 missing.

The American command was jubilant over the outcome: Westmoreland would write, 'We had soundly defeated the enemy without unduly sacrificing operations in other areas. The enemy's return was nil.' American troops had fought heroically at Dakto, air support and artillery had generally been effective, and three enemy regiments had been crippled. But in weeks to come, American intelligence noted that enemy traffic along the Ho Chi Minh Trail had doubled, and that somewhere between 20,000 and 40,000 NVA troops were gathering in the vicinity of the American firebase at Khesanh. General Giap's offensive was still gathering force.

Right: *The UH-1D (left of hut) and the heavier freight-carrying helicopters were essential to the war effort in the jungle.*

Top left: *Fast deployment from a landing zone in enemy territory prevented entrapment of troops and heavy losses to sniper fire.*

Top: *Members of the First Marine Division engage in a firefight with NVA troops, who came from the North in growing numbers to augment Vietcong efforts.*

Above: *A captured guerrilla rides with members of the 221st Signal Company en route from Cambodia to South Vietnam.*

LBJ's Peace Campaign

Soon after giving General Westmoreland a blank check to fight the war in 1965, President Johnson began to feel the heat from Congress and the public. To pacify critics and to tempt Hanoi, LBJ made a speech at Johns Hopkins University in which he offered the communists a massive pork-barrel deal: he proposed $1 billion in aid to Southeast Asia for a huge development project in the Mekong Delta. Ho Chi Minh's government, however, was not ready to be bought off. Subsequently, there were several unsuccessful diplomatic initiatives, bombing halts, and other efforts to bring Hanoi to the bargaining table. Johnson had to try and make peace with domestic dissent from both right and left and to represent the war as a matter of broad consensus and judicious policy; he made constant efforts in those directions. In February 1966, he conferred in Honolulu with South Vietnamese president Nguen Cao Ky, both of them pretending to be the happy allies they were not, as Saigon continued to rely upon the United States absolutely and to resent its powerful partner at the same time. In October LBJ flew to Manila for a conference of the seven countries that had troops fighting in Vietnam, including South Vietnam, Australia, New Zealand, South Korea, Thailand, and the Philippines. At the end of the two day conference, a joint communiqué called vainly for negotiations to end the war.

Despite such efforts, early 1967 polls showed that 57 percent of Americans disapproved of Johnson's war policy. In February of that year, LBJ sent a secret letter to Ho Chi Minh, 'in hope that the conflict in Vietnam can be brought to an end.' In his reply, the communist leader scornfully rejected Johnson's proposals: 'The Vietnamese people have never done any harm to the United States. . . . The US government has committed crimes against peace and against mankind. The Vietnamese people will never submit to force.' For some time to come, Hanoi would refuse to negotiate before a complete US pullout.

As debate raged across the country, Congress reflected all sides of the issue. The focus of the debate in Washington was the Senate Foreign Relations Committee and its powerful chairman, J William Fulbright. In February the Committee began a 'broad inquiry into Vietnam policy'. During the hearings Congressional displeasure over Johnson's highhanded attempt to fight an undeclared war was manifest, as a string of administration officials were grilled sharply. Soon afterward, Fulbright proclaimed that in pursuing the war the United States was 'succumbing to the arrogance of power.' Congressional opposition began to gather around a group of senators including Fulbright, George McGovern, Wayne Morse, and Mike Mansfield. Since Republicans favored the war, conservative voices like those of Strom Thurmond, Mendel Rivers, and Everett Dirksen had to criticize Johnson for not fighting hard enough, for refusing to mobilize the reserves or to use nuclear weapons.

Early diplomatic initiatives centered around the Christmas bombing halt of 1965, during which administration spokesmen canvassed world leaders to support American proposals for a negotiated settlement. The results were modest. In the end, the failure of the bombing halt to bring Hanoi to the table damaged the United States more than the communists. Close allies like Britain continued their official, if sometimes uneasy, support; the French had never gone along, and in fall 1966 President Charles De Gaulle called for a US withdrawal.

The mounting frustrations and ambiguities of the war fell heavily onto the shoulders of one of its prime architects: Robert

Right: *Vice-President Hubert Humphrey reports to President Johnson on his five-day diplomatic mission to the Far East in early 1966. Upon his return, Humphrey brushed aside all media questions about his trip's effect on peace in Vietnam.*

Left: *A massive protest against the war in Vietnam was held in New York City on 15 April 1967. Here demonstrators wait outside United Nations headquarters as their leaders state their cause to UN Undersecretary Ralph J Bunche. Some 125,000 Americans took part in the rally.*

Below: *Grief marks two members of the 173rd Airborne Brigade, as they await the helicopter that will take the body of a fellow soldier from the jungle of Long Khanh Province: January 1967.*

S McNamara, Secretary of Defense under both Kennedy and LBJ. Early on, he had claimed to be pleased when Wayne Morse branded the conflict 'McNamara's War.' But by 1966 the secretary's statistics were not adding up – his carefully crafted air strategy was having no discernible effect upon the supply lines or the morale of North Vietnam. Moreover, McNamara had begun to realize, as a Pentagon officer observed, 'that wars kill innocent people.' South and North Vietnamese civilians were dying under American bombs.

A year later, McNamara was visibly showing the strain. In May 1967, he recommended to the president that the air war be curtailed and troop increases limited. This ran directly counter to the policy of the Joint Chiefs, and they responded sharply. Now McNamara had parted paths not only with his president, but with his own department, and his days were numbered. In November 1967, LBJ eased out his Secretary of Defense, securing for him a position as head of the World Bank. McNamara announced his departure in a brief, tense news conference, his resignation to become effective in February 1968. However, his replacement, Clark Clifford, would prove to be far from the vigorous war manager that Johnson had hoped for.

The Siege of Khesanh

General Giap had not been discouraged by the troop losses of his opening offensive at Dakto and elsewhere; his buildup to the Tet Offensive in the cities was developing apace, and its next target was the American base at Khesanh, 14 miles below the DMZ near the Laotian border. The communists' goals in the war were always political as well as military; if the Tet Offensive failed to drive out the Americans and precipitate the fall of the South Vietnamese government, it might still bring the United States to the bargaining table. Moreover, Giap was convinced that the appearance of communist forces in the major cities of South Vietnam would engender popular uprisings against the Americans and their puppets in Saigon. In the latter, as in many aspects of the Tet Offensive, Giap miscalculated, but the results always seemed in the end to further his cause.

Westmoreland had intended the base at Khesanh as a staging area for offensives into Laos (which never developed) when the Marines seized and activated it in 1967. When intelligence reports began to show a massive NVA influx into the area – 4 divisions plus 2 artillery and 1 armored unit, totaling some 40,000 troops – Westmoreland dispatched heavy reinforcements to Khesanh and initiated the appropriately named Operation Niagara, a series of air strikes in the area that would mount to a scale unprecedented in history.

As both sides built up toward the coming explosion, the memory of Dien Bien Phu hovered over their deliberations. Were the communists trying to do what they had done to the French, besieging an isolated garrison to score a decisive military and propaganda victory? Westmoreland and especially Johnson seemed haunted by the possibility; Johnson had a model of Khesanh in the White House, which he would consult as the siege unfolded, and he snapped nervously to JCS chairman Earle Wheeler, 'I don't want any damn Dinbinphoo.'

Westmoreland knew the enemy was better armed than ever, now entirely equipped with Russian AK47 automatic rifles – considered by many the best combat rifle in the world – as well as new Soviet flamethrowers, anti-aircraft guns, rockets, and mortars. The general also knew that in contrast to the case of the French, American air power was overwhelming. As usual, that element was to make the difference at Khesanh.

At the base, Marine Colonel David E Lownds and his allied troops awaited the assault in their trenches and bunkers. Their orders were to hold Khesanh at all costs. Ringing them was an extraordinary array of state-of-the-art defenses: mines, barbed wire, razor tape, flares, acoustic sensors, seismic sensors that could feel the vibrations of advancing troops, infrared sensors, even devices that could detect human urine. In the skies, radar and scouting planes circled constantly for 30 miles in every direction. On the hills to the northeast, detachments of Marines manned outposts. An airstrip ran through the base. The men inside seemed almost to be incidental elements in a gigantic electronic game. All the same, they had plenty of things on hand with which to fight – fickle but deadly M16 automatic rifles, grenade launchers, artillery, M48 tanks, .50 caliber machine guns.

On the morning of 20 January 1968, a Marine company

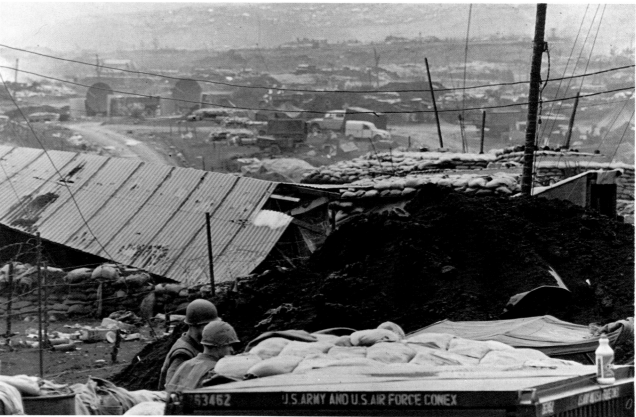

Center: *A combination of strong ground defenses and massive air support prevented the Marines and allied forces at Khesanh, just south of the DMZ, from suffering the fate of French forces at Dien Bien Phu.*

Right: *Marines inspect a sandbagged area at their Khesanh base, seized from the enemy the previous year, during the nine-week siege of early 1968.*

Far right: *Extensive trenches and bunkers helped enable the 6000 defenders of Khesanh to resist NVA forces far superior in number. The American public watched the entire siege on television, along with numerous other battles of the Tet Offensive. Support for the war eroded rapidly.*

patrolling Hill 881 near Khesanh was hit by a hail of enemy fire that felled 20 men in seconds. The battle was on. Alerted to enemy plans by an NVA defector, Colonel Lownds pulled the company back and awaited the initial shelling he had been told to expect. It arrived as predicted, just after midnight – a mortar, rocket, and grenade barrage falling on the outpost at Hill 861. Some 300 elite NVA soldiers followed, broaching the defensive wire briefly before a Marine counterattack drove them back in hand-to-hand fighting. As Hill 861 quieted down, heavy mortar fire began falling on Khesanh, detonating a big ammunition dump near the airstrip and sending helicopters rolling around the base. Shells from the smoldering dump were exploding into the next day. Another enemy round hit some tear gas canisters, blanketing Khesanh in choking fumes.

Within a few days, a Marine and an ARVN battalion arrived by air, to raise the number of defenders to 6000 men; all of them spent most of their time huddled in bunkers under the incessant shelling, which at its peak on 23 February amounted to 1300 incoming rounds. Despite heavy enemy anti-aircraft fire in the area, Westmoreland ordered Niagara II into motion. For the next 9 weeks, B-52s and other planes dropped 100,000 tons of bombs around Khesanh, in addition to the 150,000 artillery rounds dropped onto the enemy. Together, the combined explosive power of this American barrage was equivalent to five Hiroshima-sized atomic bombs hitting the narrow perimeter around the base. The communists died in thousands under this incredible rain of steel and fire, but the siege continued.

In late January, General Giap arrived at Khesanh to take charge personally – just as he had done at Dien Bien Phu. But by then the siege was about to become a sideshow to Giap's Tet Offensive, which broke out all over South Vietnam on 30

Left: *Defenders watch smoke billowing from a fuel dump after a Vietcong mortar attack late in the siege. Some 10,000 North Vietnamese were killed at Khesanh, as against 500 American casualties.*

Below: *Marine forward observers try to spot the elusive enemy and get a fix on his mortar positions from front lines in February 1968.*

Top left: *A Marine lance corporal armed with an M-14 fires at an enemy forward observer outside the Khesanh perimeter.*

Left: *Marines at Khesanh wait out an enemy artillery barrage in their trenches, rifles ready to counter the ground assault that may follow.*

January. Perhaps because of the fighting elsewhere, the expected big ground attack on Khesanh never arrived. For the Marines, the seige was a daily affair of 'waitin' and diggin'. Around the world, the public watched it all on television.

The outlying bases also took their share of communist bombardment, but on 7 February a new threat materialized: at the Lang Vei Special Forces camp, Russian-made NVA tanks attacked for the first time in the war. Three tanks were disabled by American artillery and air fire, but two more broke into the camp to fire pointblank into bunkers and gun emplacements. By morning, Lang Vei was leveled, only a few survivors escaping to Khesanh. Most of the 200 dead and missing at the camp were Civilian Irregular Defense Group fighters; 10 US Marines were also killed.

On 1 April, after the Tet Offensive had wound down, General Westmoreland launched Operation Pegasus to relieve Khesanh. The plan was for the 1st Cavalry to mount an air assault east of the base while two Marine divisions advanced along Route 9. At the same time, defenders in the base began to push the enemy back. It went as planned: on 6 April the cavalrymen linked up with Marines from the base south of the airstrip, and the siege was over. A week later, however, Marines had two more days of brutal fighting before they could dislodge the last NVA troops from Hill 471 on Route 9.

Khesanh left many questions in its wake. The NVA had lost perhaps 10,000 men killed during the siege, compared to 500 Americans. (Most of the slaughter of the enemy was the work of American B-52 strikes.) What was the strategic purpose that led

Above: *The airstrip at Khesanh – which had been seized as a staging base for operations into nearby Laos that never materialized – enabled both supply and evacuation of the besieged outpost.*

Giap to sanction such appalling losses? Westmoreland believed that Khesanh was the real target of the communist offensive, and that the wide-ranging Tet operation was essentially a diversion. After the war, NVA commanders would insist that Khesanh was never expected to be a repeat of Dien Bien Phu, but was rather the diversion for Tet, and a successful one – it drew American forces away from the South, leaving the cities open to the main offensive. Historians have not settled the question of whether the siege was a successful feint or a strategic mistake by the communists.

As for Khesanh itself, its end was sudden and inglorious: two months after the battle, the base that Westmoreland had called the most critical of all was razed and abandoned by the Marines. An American commander explained the departure to an incredulous press: 'To defeat an enemy, you've got to keep moving. We're through sitting in one place and taking our lumps.' The communists walked into Khesanh and reclaimed it.

Top right: *Fire was an ever-present hazard at Khesanh due to the severity of enemy rocket and mortar attacks.*

Center, left: *The wreckage of a C-130 transport plane shot down by the NVA during a resupply mission.*

Above: *A flame tank sprays lethal napalm toward enemy positions.*

Left: *US Air Force F-4s provided close air support at Khesanh, while B-52 bombing strikes accounted for most of the heavy NVA casualties.*

Following pages: *ARVN Rangers patrol the Cholon section of Saigon after the Tet Offensive.*

119

PART III

A Full-blown War

The Tet Offensive

General Vo Nguyen Giap's general offensive in the border battles including Khesanh were only a preparation for the main communist attacks scheduled to begin on the first day of Tet – the sacred celebration of the Lunar New Year, during which there had traditionally been a ceasefire. The offensive was scheduled for that time partly for surprise value, but also because for the history-minded communists it was the anniversary of a legendary Tet battle of 1789, when the emperor of Vietnam drove the Chinese from Hanoi. On the eve of the operation, Radio Hanoi broadcast a poem written for the occasion by Ho Chi Minh: 'This spring far outshines the previous springs,/ Of victories throughout the land come happy tidings./ Let North and South emulate each other in fighting the United States aggressors!/ Forward! Total victory will be ours!'

As always, the US MACV command had been monitoring enemy movements with its sophisticated network of intelligence sources, ranging from spies to electronic bugs scattered around the countryside to airborne surveillance. The trouble was that all this intelligence, flowing in from various branches of the military and CIA, constantly generated mountains of data that were hard to grasp and interpret. As a result, commanders tended to find in the data what they wanted to find. In Decem-

Top: *Combined mortar and rocket attack on Tan Son Nhut Airbase.*

Above: *Searching out snipers.*

Right: *A Marine stands ready to use his M-79 grenade launcher during the surprise Tet Offensive of 1968.*

ber, as the border battles heated up, American intelligence clearly indicated that something big was in the wind: Joint Chiefs chairman Earle Wheeler predicted 'a communist thrust similar to the desperate effort of the Germans in World War II.' Westmoreland alerted Washington that a 'maximum effort' was coming from the enemy and ordered reinforcements into Saigon; at the same time, he assured Washington that the enemy were on their last legs. As Tet approached, the South Vietnamese government was even more sanguine. New president Nguyen Van Thieu dispensed furloughs to most ARVN troops and left Saigon for the holiday.

Thus the real scope and thrust of the communist campaign fell through the cracks of the vast US intelligence network. Westmoreland believed that the Khesanh attack was the climax, an attempt by Hanoi to seize control of the border area. Others disagreed, but no allied commander suspected that Vietcong and North Vietnamese Army troops in the South numbered some 80,000; this was no desperate last-ditch attempt, but a gigantic offensive by a fighting force at the peak of its strength and morale. Later, military historians would describe the United States intelligence debacle of that period as a 'failure ranking with Pearl Harbor.'

The Tet Offensive exploded into action in the early morning of 30 January 1968, with attacks on a string of cities – Nha Trang, Ban Me Thuot, Kontum, Hoi An, Danang, Quinhon, Pleiku. As fighting surged through those cities, MACV command tried to

figure out what was happening. The next day, when complete hell broke loose, the map in the Saigon US operations center lit up like a Christmas tree: the communists were striking all over South Vietnam – at the 9 largest cities'and 30 provincial capitals.

The boldest effort, because it would have the maximum psychological impact, fell on Saigon. Enemy operations in the capital of South Vietnam reflected most of the techniques that were used during the Tet Offensive. Over several weeks, some 4000 VC had infiltrated Saigon dressed as farmers, fruit vendors, tourists, and the like, carrying their weapons in innocent-looking packages. Other arms and supplies arrived in truckloads of rice and vegetables, slipping easily past lax ARVN security posts.

An elite group of commandos, part of the Vietcong C10 Sapper Battalion, was assigned to the most telling Saigon objective of all: at 2:45 AM on 31 January, a plastic charge blew a hole through the high concrete wall protecting the American Embassy and nineteen men slipped into the compound. Over the radio, MACV command heard an American MP screaming, 'They're coming in! They're coming in! Help me! Help me!' Then the radio went dead. The enemy had penetrated the *sanctum sanctorum* of the American presence in Vietnam.

An hour earlier, another unit of the Sapper Battalion had blasted through the gate of the presidential palace, shouting 'We are the Liberation Army!' They were quickly driven back by the guards, but it took two days of fighting to root them out of

Above: *Troops of the 6th Infantry Division take cover during fierce fighting in Cholon, the Chinese sector of Saigon.*

Top left: *An Armored Personnel Carrier takes the road toward an area held by the enemy.*

Left: *Shattered vehicles, tree limbs, and panels of corrugated iron litter the street outside US Bachelor Officers' Quarters in Saigon in the wake of a Vietcong attack during Tet.*

Left: US Ambassador Ellsworth Bunker (partially hidden by MP's rifle) inspects damage to the grounds of the US Embassy in Saigon on 31 January 1968.

Below: A wounded Vietcong infiltrator and a communist nurse who surrendered during street fighting in Cholon are escorted by ARVN Rangers.

the street. In contrast, at the American Embassy the commandos roamed the compound, shooting away with their automatic weapons and sending anti-tank rockets through the locked doors of the chancery building. At the outset there were only three Marines inside to stand up to the VC; two MPs had died in the first moments of the attack, although they had apparently gunned down some of the leaders first and blunted the assault.

As the VC tried to find a way into the chancery, American troops began to arrive. By the time 36 heliborne soldiers landed on the chancery roof, all 19 commandos had been killed or captured; senior embassy official Colonel George Jacobson shot the last one as he was coming up the chancery stairs. Seven Marines had been killed in the six hours of shooting. That night on television, shocked millions saw the aftermath on film: soldiers and embassy officials including Ambassador Ellsworth Bunker walking grimly around the rubble of the compound, inspecting the bodies of dead guerrillas. That indelible image had much to do with the later course of public opinion, but worse images were to come.

Another contingent of the VC Sapper Battalion had more luck – briefly – in their objective of capturing the National Radio Station, from which they intended to broadcast calls for a civilian uprising against the South Vietnamese government. Disguised as local riot police, 20 sappers expertly blasted their way into the station compound and annihilated a surprised platoon of guards. But before the VC could gain the control room, a technician sent out a signal to shut down the transmitter. Planned communist reinforcements failed to arrive, and the commandos were finally trapped in the station as ARVN troops gathered outside. A few hours later, all were shot when they tried to escape after setting the building on fire.

The communists fanned out through Saigon, pursued by ARVN and American detachments, news cameramen and reporters close behind. Near the An Quang temple, photographers were on hand to record what would become one of the most horrifying images of the war. On the nightly news, the world was to see a captured VC guerrilla, a small, stolid man with his hands bound, wearing a checkered sport shirt, led up

Above: *Members of Company A, 30th Ranger Battalion, maintain radio contact as they advance toward Vietcong terrorists around Saigon on the first day of Tet.*

Left: *Marines take shelter behind a battered wall during the costly street-to-street fight for Hué, the ancient capital of Vietnam.*

Above and left: The Vietcong attack on the US Embassy. The rocket hole in the reinforced wall admitted 19 Vietcong commandos to the grounds of the compound, all of whom were captured or killed within six hours. Seven Marines and two MPs who defended the embassy died in the fighting.

Top right: One of the Vietcong casualties of the attack on the US Embassy: 31 January 1968.

Right: US infantrymen search a Saigon cemetery for snipers.

to General Nguyen Ngoc Loan, chief of the South Vietnamese National Police. It happened very quickly, but viewers seem to remember it in slow motion: Loan raises a small silver gun to the head of the helpless man and pulls the trigger; a crack, the man's head recoils from the blast, he falls kicking, the blood spurts in a ghastly torrent from his head. In that single event, war came into the living rooms of the world with all its violence.

Throughout January 31st, fighting raged in and around Saigon. A massive early-morning VC attack fell on the Tan Son Nhut airbase, which contained MACV headquarters. The South Vietnamese Army staff headquarters and other military installations were also hit, the operations meticulously planned and executed. Elsewhere, VC cadres searched buildings and herded civilians into the streets, holding 'people's courts' to try enemies from prepared lists and proclaiming the 'liberation' of Saigon. Some civilians and off-duty ARVN were summarily shot. But the popular uprising that General Giap had predicted

would support the Vietcong never materialized; without that, the entire offensive was foredoomed by superior American/ARVN numbers and firepower.

Over the next days, some 10,000 ARVN soldiers and National Police began to sweep through the city, isolating pockets of enemy resistance and mopping them up. Starting on 4 February, air strikes tore at the last holdouts, especially at the Phu Tho racetrack, killing the enemy and South Vietnamese civilians alike. The 80 separate engagements that made up the battle of Saigon ended on the 10th, when US infantry secured the racetrack in hand-to-hand fighting.

Elsewhere around South Vietnam, the story of the Tet Offensive was similar: a quick seizure of key points by enemy infiltrators and a deadly but inexorable process of dislodging them by ARVN and American forces. At Quang Ngai City, the fighting was over in eight hours; at Pleiku it went on for eight days. But the most extended and brutal Tet battle raged through the old imperial capital of Hué.

The Battle for Hué

There was no lovelier city in Vietnam than Hué, capital of Thua Thien Province and the former imperial capital. The religious and cultural center of the entire country, it was a city of exotic palaces and temples, with a population proud and cosmopolitan. Through the middle runs the Perfume River, north of which lies the gigantic fortress of the Imperial Citadel, built by the emperor in 1802. Within its moat and 6 miles of encircling walls, 20 feet thick and 30 feet high, were 2 square miles of elegant boulevards and a maze of defensive positions and inner walls. Inevitably, Hué was a primary target of the communist Tet Offensive, for both military and symbolic reasons, and the Citadel was their first objective.

As everywhere in the opening of the Tet Offensive, the communist attack on Hué achieved virtually complete surprise. In the early morning of 31 January 1968, 5000 North Vietnamese Army infiltrators inside the city changed into their uniforms and started shooting, while a three-pronged attack by 7000 more NVA troops hit the city from the outside, meeting little resistance from the ARVN guarding the Citadel. On the south bank of the Perfume River, the enemy surrounded the US MACV headquarters, occupied by only 200 Americans.

In a short time, the American and ARVN compounds had been isolated and communist forces were sweeping through the city at will. Dawn of 1 February revealed the blue and red flag of the National Liberation Front flying over the Citadel. The American command at the nearby Marine base of Phubai was slow to react, at first sending only a company to relieve the city. That column was soon calling for help. With reinforcements, the Marines fought their way to the MACV compound; over the next three days they would be joined by 1000 more troops. By that time, the communists were firmly in position on both sides of the river. Their armory and barracks was the old Quoc Hoc High School, among whose notable former students were Ngo Dinh Diem, Vo Nguyen Giap, and Ho Chi Minh.

Above: *A US Marine fires an M-79 grenade launcher from his fighting hole on the south bank of the Perfume River at communist positions on the north bank: Hué, February 1968.*

Left: *A Marine observation plane makes a low-level pass over the ruins of Hué during the Tet Offensive.*

While the allies organized their forces and pondered how to get the enemy out of Hué, the communists unleashed an unprecedented campaign of terror in the city. From a hit list prepared months before, squads of young NVA guerrillas began moving from house to house, arresting those branded 'cruel tyrants and reactionary elements.' Most of those rounded up were South Vietnamese government functionaries; others included French priests, a German doctor and his family, an American employee of the United States Information Service, even a part-time janitor at a government office.

In the months after the battle, these people would be found in mass graves at scattered locations around the city: they had been shot, strangled, beaten to death, sometimes buried alive. No one will ever know the true extent of communist atrocities· in Hué. Some of the graves were never found, and after the battle ARVN Political Warfare units moved in and added to the graves some of their own assassinations, visited on suspected communist collaborators. The victims probably numbered somewhere between 3000 and 5000. But the ultimate effect of the atrocities amounted to another miscalculation by the communist planners of Tet: more than anything else, the massacre of civilians at Hué led to the conviction that a North Vietnamese victory in the war would lead to a massive bloodbath. For some time to come, that conviction considerably strengthened the resolve of both the ARVN and the Americans.

The allies were outnumbered at Hué, but as always, they had enormous superiority in materiel. There were enough howitzers, recoilless rifles, helicopter gunships, fighter-bombers, and offshore naval vessels with their big guns to level the city entirely. Before long, however, the American command realized it was going to have to be primarily a ground fight:

slogging street-to-street, house-to-house, flushing out the enemy hand-to-hand – the most grueling and savage kind of fighting.

At the outset, American forces were assigned to clear the south bank of the river while the ARVN operated out of their compound in the Citadel. One Marine commander recalled, 'We were new to this type of situation. We were accustomed to jungles and open rice fields, and now we would be fighting in a city, like it was Europe during World War II ... we were going to take a number of casualties learning some basic lessons in this experience.' While learning those lessons, it took a Marine unit the better part of a week to fight four blocks from the MACV compound to their objective, a hospital. Teams would move from house to house, four men covering the exits while two others tossed in grenades and two more provided covering fire. 'It sounds simple,' one Marine observed of the deadly game, 'but the timing has to be just as good as a football play.' Often, the local commander would find it safer and more efficient simply to blow the house away with artillery.

As this agonizing fighting ground on, MACV command began to pull in forces for a major assault. In the middle of February, the 1st Air Cavalry and 101st Airborne began moving toward the Citadel from the west while other units crossed the river from the south bank, which finally had been cleared. By that point ARVN inside the Citadel had gained control of the northern half, including the airport, but the communists were strongly dug in over the rest. As the Marines poured in to join the ARVN in the Citadel, the full range of American air, ground, and naval forces shelled the communist positions, but that did not alleviate the bitterness of the ground fighting. 'On the worst days,' said a correspondent, 'no one expected to get through it alive. A despair

Top left: *The fight for Phu Thu Racetrack near the Chinese quarter was one of the bitterest of 80 separate engagements during the Tet battle for Saigon.*

Left: *The battle-scarred Shrine of the Warrior, Hué.*

Above: *A Marine of the 1st Regiment takes cover behind a tree to return fire from a North Vietnamese position during street fighting in Hué.*

set in among members of the battalion that the older ones, veterans of two other wars, had never seen before.' It was estimated that there was one Marine casualty for every yard gained. With reinforcements scarce, many men were fighting 20 hours a day. Soldiers began to take on the hollow-eyed, empty look that had been called during World War II 'the thousand-yard stare.'

The Marines crawled through the rubble, past the decomposing bodies of friends, enemies, and civilians, past groups of residents huddling in ruins or searching for food. Enemy snipers were as pervasive as the ghastly smell of death. Artillery and air strikes often had to be directed only yards away· from friendly troops to dislodge the NVA from a strongpoint; otherwise, enemy pockets had to be handled with grenades and rifle fire. In a crazy counterpoint, roaring loudspeakers manned by the opposing sides, only yards apart, proclaimed victory and called for support from the devastated population. But one student voiced the prevailing civilian attitude – 'We don't care about anything except rice. We know well the VC. We know well the Americans. We want to go to our homes and not be afraid of being killed by either side.' A great many had no homes left to return to.

Around 16 February the NVA commander in the Citadel was killed and his replacement asked for permission to withdraw. The request was denied, but the enemy clearly had had enough. On the morning of the 24th, an ARVN division overran the south wall and raised the South Vietnamese flag over the Citadel. That night the remaining communists fled. Hanoi's great Tet Offensive had run its course.

For devastated Hué, the agony would continue: half the city was damaged or destroyed, over three-quarters of the population was homeless, some 5800 civilians had been killed. The graves of the assassinated were being discovered and after the battle the citizens had to watch the final humiliation – ARVN and American soldiers looting the ruins of their homes. Casualties in the fighting were, as usual, utterly disproportionate: over 5000 communists had been killed, 89 captured; the Marines had lost 142 dead and 857 wounded; other US troops, 74 killed and 507 wounded; ARVN casualties were 384 killed and 1830 wounded.

The 1st Marines amply earned their subsequent presidential citation for 'effective teamwork, aggressive fighting spirit and individual acts of heroism and daring.' A World War II general once observed, however, that when a country's own troops fight hard it is called heroism; when the enemy fights hard, it is called fanaticism. Time and again, the Vietnamese Communists proved themselves as tough and resourceful as any soldiers in the world, and their commanders were willing to sacrifice any number of casualties to further their long-range goals. The aftermath of Tet showed the soundness of that cold-blooded strategy.

In Washington and Saigon, the process of evaluating the Tet Offensive began: the body counts, the losses in territory and materiel, the ultimate question of who won and who lost. The answer to the latter question would prove to be very different on the battlefield and in the equally important realm of public opinion.

Above: *Residents of Hué begin sifting through the wreckage of their homes for personal belongings on 27 February, after South Vietnamese troops had blasted through a gate of the Imperial Palace to win the 25-day battle for the former capital.*

Right: *Marines patrol the rubble-strewn streets of Hué in the shadow of the Old City's battered tower: late February 1968.*

The Aftermath of Tet

In the massive offensives across South Vietnam that raged from September 1967 to the end of February 1968, the communists played nearly every card in their hands. They had hoped to gain a stunning military victory, or failing that, to initiate a popular uprising against the South Vietnamese government and to demonstrate the vulnerability of the American war machine. In practice, the campaign achieved none of those things.

The North Vietnamese Army and the Vietcong had suffered terrible casualties – some 50,000 dead and many times that number wounded. Later an official communist report would confess, 'we did not correctly evaluate the specific balance of forces between ourselves and the enemy, did not fully realize that the enemy still had considerable capabilities and that our capabilities were limited . . . [our objectives] were beyond our actual strength . . . we suffered large losses in materiel and manpower . . . which clearly weakened us.' For once, the barrage of statistics that Westmoreland gave to the press really reflected a significant battlefield victory for the allies and a genuine blow at Hanoi's strength and morale. Moreover, the new CIA covert program, 'Phoenix', would severely damage the communists' vital rural infrastructure in 1968 with a Vietcong-style campaign of persuasion, terror, and assassination.

When all was said and done, Tet proved to be the turning point of the war. The sublime irony of the outcome was that it turned the war in favor of the communists. If wars were fought entirely on the battlefield, that would not have been the case, but they are inescapably political as well, and it was on the political stage that America lost the Tet battles and the war.

The American people had been stunned and sickened by televised images of the fighting: the bodies in the United States Embassy in Saigon, the shooting of a helpless captive by a police chief, the fighting at Khesanh and Hué, the surrealistic observation of an American major as his men burned Ben Tre: 'It became necessary to destroy the town in order to save it.' Watching the films, popular TV newsman Walter Cronkite reacted like millions of Americans: 'What the hell is going on? I thought we were winning the war.' Political satirist Art Buchwald produced a column headed 'We Have the Enemy on the Run, Says General Custer at Little Big Horn.'

By portraying the communists as beaten and near collapse for so long, US commanders had sown the seeds of disaster. Tet convinced the world that American military optimism had been a lie or a delusion, and millions would never trust the government's rosy statistics and predictions again. The Johnson administration did its best to handle the wave of disillusionment and rage that swept the country; advisor Walt Rostow managed a 'Success Offensive' that inundated the media with stories of victory and hope. It did no good. Opinion polls showed a sharp upturn in those dissatisfied with the war, and for the first time the number of doves and hawks in Congress was almost equal.

Right: *An anxious President Johnson, left, studies a model of the Marine base at Khesanh in the White House situation room with two advisors.*

Below left: *A US Army M-48 tank crippled by a land mine near Cu Chi.*

Below: *Refugees from North Vietnam display a flag proclaiming their solidarity with the South Vietnamese Army during the pacification period that followed Tet.*

It was the political events of February and March 1968 that finally destroyed Lyndon Johnson's dreams of victory. General Westmoreland asked for 206,000 more troops and insisted on calling up the reserves; instead, Johnson deferred a decision and asked new Defense Secretary Clark Clifford to review national policy. During consultations with military leaders, Clifford found to his dismay that the United States had only one military goal – attrition, or killing as many communists as possible – and that communist strength had increased immensely during the years of American engagement. Clifford responded by forming an underground movement within the government to promote disengagement and bluntly told LBJ the war was 'a real loser.' Johnson then convened a council of distinguished advisors dubbed the 'Wise Men' in hopes of gaining support for further escalation; instead, they advised that the United States seek peace negotiations. General Westmoreland was relieved from Vietnam duty in June to become chairman of the Joint Chiefs of Staff, his successor being General Creighton Abrams. It was a clear signal that Washington was turning away from the strategies Westmoreland had represented.

Johnson's political decline became dramatically visible in March, when anti-war senator Eugene McCarthy emerged from obscurity to run a close second to the president in the New Hampshire Democratic primary. Soon after, Senator Robert Kennedy announced that he would run and would oppose the war. No one had more sensitive political antennae than Johnson, and what they sensed boded very ill indeed.

On 31 March 1968, Johnson went on television to announce that he had ordered a halt to most air and naval bombardments of North Vietnam in hopes of negotiations. In his final words, which not even his closest advisors knew were coming, he star-

tled the world: 'I have concluded that I should not permit the presidency to become involved in the partisan divisions that are developing in this political year. Accordingly, I shall not seek, and I will not accept, the nomination of my party for another term as your president.' LBJ had become a casualty of his own war.

The ensuing months of that political year were among the darkest in American history. In early April the great civil rights leader Martin Luther King Jr was assassinated in Tennessee. Two months later, candidate Robert Kennedy was fatally shot in California. The year's political conventions took place amid a climate of deep unrest at home and extensive new communist offensives in Vietnam. Richard Nixon won the Republican nomination, pledging to 'bring an honorable end to the war.' At the Democratic National Convention in Chicago, Vice-President Hubert Humphrey took the nomination, pledging lamely to continue Johnson's policies of de-escalation. Outside the hall, over 10,000 demonstrators battled with police, climaxing the 221 major anti-war demonstrations of 1968. It was as if the war had jumped from Vietnam to the streets of the United States: was society coming apart?

Loyal to his old friend and mentor Johnson, Humphrey refused until late in the campaign to distance himself from the president's policies; meanwhile, Nixon proclaimed a 'secret plan to end the war.' That plan never materialized, and Nixon was to pursue the war as long as LBJ, but in 1968 the American people were ready to listen to any promise of peace. Despite the genial Humphrey's personal popularity, and considerable suspicion of the cold and secretive Nixon, the Republicans took the election. The course of the Nixon administration, however, was only to deepen the malaise of the United States.

Massacre at My Lai

Top left: *President Johnson decorates a young soldier during a 1967 trip to Vietnam aimed partly at shoring up declining troop morale.*

Above: *Lt. William Calley (center, with attorney) returns to Vietnam in 1970 to face charges of mass murder in the 1968 My Lai massacre.*

There is a certain point in warfare when the soldiers who are losing begin to act like beaten men. The results are variable, depending upon the culture and the situation: in World War II, for example, the prospect of defeat only made the Japanese fight more ferociously, to the point of suicide. In the case of American servicemen in Vietnam, there was a growing sense of rage and frustration throughout 1968. That fact, coupled with a steady decline in the quality of incoming troops (by then many of America's better educated young men were avoiding service), produced a formula for atrocity.

American war crimes were generally free-lance affairs; unlike the atrocities of Germany in World War II and of the communists in Vietnam, they were not a component of military strategy at the highest level. Of course, the peasants who found themselves being uprooted, tortured, raped, and murdered, cared little about which side or which level of command was responsible for their suffering. And the peasants of Vietnam suffered and died to the number of more than 400,000. Almost a million civilians were wounded.

For American troops, village operations were among the most dreaded of assignments. The communists used the villages and hamlets regularly, hiding in the houses of peasants whether or not they were true allies. A US company might arrive at a formerly friendly village to find devastating fire erupting from the huts; then the enemy would disappear when

the Americans fought their way in. This was the experience of a platoon from Charlie Company of the 20th Infantry Brigade. During patrols in Vietcong-filled Quang Ngai Province, they had been steadily eroded by booby traps, snipers, and mines, without ever finding anyone to shoot at. By 16 March 1968, when the platoon was ordered to attack a Vietcong battalion said to be at My Lai-4, the young American soldiers were ready to explode. Charlie Company captain Ernest L Medina told his men that they were about to 'get even' with the enemy. His instructions implied that all the villagers were to be killed.

What followed was utter savagery. The infantrymen advanced into the village shooting, although there was no opposing fire, few rifles were in evidence, and no stores of enemy weapons were found. Nonetheless, the villagers – old, young, male, female – were systematically shot, bayoneted, and beaten to death. Two girls were raped before being killed; old women were shot in the head as they prayed desperately at an altar. The butchery climaxed when Lieutenant William L Calley ordered his men to herd some 150 civilians into a drainage ditch, where they were mowed down by automatic-weapons fire. Finally, some 400 people lay dead. The only US casualty was a soldier who had shot himself in the foot. Captain Medina reported 128 of the enemy killed and later received a special commendation for the day's action.

The My Lai incident was not unique in the war. Such atrocities verged on standard operating procedure for the communists, and there were other such slaughters by American and ARVN troops in addition to the regular use of torture in interrogations. On the same day as My Lai, for example, a similar massacre of 90 civilians was carried out at nearby My Khe-4.

What made My Lai different was its scale, the absence of communist forces – and the fact that news photographers were on hand to record the horror. Medina, Calley, and their men were so blood-crazed that they did not even think to stop the newsmen from taking pictures. Over a year later, the pictures materialized in American magazines: mounds of bodies, terrified women and children looking into the gunbarrels of Charlie Company during their last seconds of life. Americans had seen pictures of this kind before, but the villains had been Nazis or communists. This time it was their own boys who were raping and killing the innocent. It was too terrible to believe, but the evidence was irrefutable. Journalist Seymour Hersh would win a Pulitzer Prize for his account of the massacre.

In time-honored fashion, the American military did its best to cover up the My Lai incident. When it finally leaked out, the same tradition protected the higher ranking officers involved in the coverup and picked out a few scapegoats to throw to the wolves. A couple of generals were censured and demoted, but Calley was the only soldier convicted of anything: neither well educated nor experienced, he was the ideal scapegoat. (After Calley's court martial in 1971, he spent only a few years in jail, although his original sentence of life imprisonment had been commuted to 20 years.)

My Lai and other atrocities showed that the American ground war was falling apart; when morale and leadership go bad, it is the beginning of the end. An Army colonel observed, 'We have at least two or three thousand Calleys in the army just waiting for the next calamity.' And a senior general explained that he had turned against Vietnam because 'I will be damned if I will permit the United States Army, its institutions, its doctrines, and its traditions to be destroyed just to win this lousy war.'

The War Continues in the Field

In the tumultuous month of March 1968, during which the Tet Offensive was winding down, the My Lai atrocities took place, and LBJ announced he would step down, General Creighton W Abrams was named head of the Military Assistance Command, Vietnam, replacing General William Westmoreland. Abrams was to take command in July. In contrast to the courtly Westmoreland, 'Abe' Abrams was a tough, cigar-chewing, profane old fighter who, it was said, 'likes to hit the enemy . . . and stay with them until he has killed every one of them.'

Abrams knew well, however, that Johnson was ready to wind down the war. The half-million American troops already in Vietnam were to be increased by some 25,000, but that was far less than the 206,000 that Westmoreland had asked for to pursue the war effectively. The task of the new MACV commander was to prepare for a negotiated peace and an American pullout. In other words, Abrams had to carry out the galling assignment of not winning a war.

As Abrams prepared to take over, Westmoreland's last operations reflected his preferred large-scale style. One of them was the biggest of the war – the optimistically named Operation Toan Thang (Total Victory). Carried out during April-May 1968,

it involved 42 American and 37 ARVN battalions, a total of over 100,000 men. The objective was to destroy enemy forces around Saigon, as part of Westmoreland's post-Tet counteroffensive. The units of Toan Thang spread out over Gia Dinh Province in small search-and-destroy patrols as well as larger daylight missions and cordon maneuvers. The net gain was impressive – over 7600 communists killed. Beginning at the same time but going on through November, Operation Burlington Trail swept through Quang Tri Province and accounted for 1931 enemy fatalities.

The main event of the allied counteroffensive was Operation Delaware/Lam Son 216, a raid into the Ashau Valley in Thua Thien Province, near the Laotian border. There lay the most important North Vietnamese Army stronghold in South Vietnam – the center from which the Tet attacks on the northern provinces had been launched. Although garrisoned by only five to six thousand NVA troops, the Ashau Valley was ringed by a formidable wall of anti-aircraft installations.

General William B Rosson planned a multifaceted attack: after six days of B-52 strikes, the 1st Air Cavalry and the ARVN 6th Airborne were to ferry troops in by helicopter; the ARVN would

Right: *Men of the 11th Armored Cavalry are pinned down by sniper fire at Long Dinh in April 1968.*

Bottom left: *A Marine machine gunner and his team leader on patrol south of Danang.*

Below: An M-48 tank and its crew escape unscathed after the detonation of a land mine in the road.

then sweep from the east over the hills while American forces moved southeast down the valley. The waves of helicopters began taking off in miserably wet weather on 19 April. Besides the clouds that obscured landing zones, pilots had to contend with enemy anti-aircraft fire, which downed 10 helicopters on the first day alone. What should have been a short hop became, as one general observed, 'an hour and 20 minutes of stark terror' in the air.

Slowly the allied troops gained a foothold and began moving on the ground. When the weather cleared in late April, the big CH-47 Chinook helicopters began bringing in artillery to shell the valley from high ground. The communist garrison declined to stand and fight; instead, they retreated into the hills to harass the allies with mortar and artillery fire. By the time Delaware/Lam Son wound up in mid-May, only 850 NVA had been killed, while 139 Americans were dead and some 60 helicopters damaged or destroyed. On the other hand, a mountain of enemy materiel was captured, including over 2000 small arms, dozens of machine guns, and 13 anti-aircraft guns, plus rocket launchers, explosives, recoilless rifles, a tank, various other vehicles, and a great deal of ammunition. With good reason, General Rosson called his operation 'one of the most audacious, skillfully executed, and successful combat undertakings of the Vietnam War.'

Marine campaigns during Westmoreland's last months in Vietnam included Operation Scotland II, which went on for nearly a year in the Khesanh area and accounted for an estimated 3311 enemy dead, and Operation Allen Brook in southern Quang Nam Province, which killed 1017 communists. Drained as they were by the Tet Offensive and Westmoreland's counteroffensive, however, the communists were still able to unleash another wide-ranging campaign in early May 1968.

Previous pages: *Cavalrymen and paratroopers team up for ground fighting against entrenched NVA and Vietcong forces north of Bien Hoa.* **Inset:** *Taking cover during a fire fight.*

Above: *Diplomat Henry A Kissinger briefs reporters at the White House on recent attempts to negotiate a cease-fire with North Vietnam.*

Below: *Operation Somerset Plain, A Shau Valley, August 1968.*

The Paris Peace Talks Begin

In the spring of 1968, President Johnson had finally been persuaded that negotiations were the only answer. Soon after his 31 March announcement of a partial bombing halt over North Vietnam (the same speech in which he announced he would not run again), Hanoi agreed to meet with the United States, much to everyone's surprise. Johnson appointed a group of old diplomatic hands to his negotiating team, which was initially headed by W Averell Harriman. Veteran Hanoi diplomat Xuan Thuy headed the communist delegation. It was agreed that the talks would be held in Paris.

At first, the talks were entirely between the Americans and the North Vietnamese; the South Vietnamese government was not included, and neither was the National Liberation Front, the political arm of the Vietcong. South Vietnamese President Nguyen Van Thieu refused for a time to deal in any way with the NLF and insisted that the United States keep up military pressure. Johnson reassured his ally that this would be done.

The first formal session opened in Paris on 13 May, when Xuan Thuy started a war of words, accusing the United States of 'monstrous crimes' and demanding a total cessation of bombing of North Vietnam before talks could proceed. Impasse set in immediately. In December, South Vietnamese and NLF delegations joined the talks, which began inauspiciously with an absurd wrangle over the shape of the negotiating table, with all parties refusing any seating arrangement that seemed to give precedence to any faction. Finally, having settled on a circular table, the delegates quickly deadlocked again despite a temporary US bombing halt.

After months without progress, the new US president, Richard M Nixon, directed his national security advisor, Henry Kissinger, to begin secret talks in Paris with Xuan Thuy. It was these talks that would, much later, lead to a breakthrough. Even as he began them, however, Kissinger was supporting a top-

secret plan for an enormous military escalation against North Vietnam, to lend weight to American bargaining power. For the United States and Vietnam alike, the negotiations were to prove yet another prolongation of the agony.

Above: *A ponderous M48-A3 tank is pulled out of the mud by Armored Personnel Carriers of the 1st Cavalry during field operations in the summer of 1968.*

Left: *Marines climb Mutters Ridge just south of the DMZ.*

The Communists Take the Offensive Again

Although they had been severely hurt during the Tet Offensive of early 1968, the communists were determined to keep up the pressure on the South. This strategy was partly intended to prove that General Westmoreland had been wrong in calling the Tet Offensive a desperate, final gamble; more importantly, Hanoi wanted to make a show of strength as the Paris peace talks began. As usual, in this offensive Hanoi would choose the time and place to fight.

What came to be called 'Tet II' broke out on 5 May 1968, when units composed primarily of NVA began shelling 119 cities, towns, and barracks in South Vietnam. Most of the attacks were really a matter of harassment with rockets and mortars – deadly enough, but no real military threat. In a few places, however, there was bitter ground fighting, and again, the capital was a focus of enemy efforts. The second battle of Saigon commenced with communist shells falling into the heart of the city. Ground forces followed, closing a major bridge and attacking the Tan Son Nhut airport, from which American troops drove the enemy in heavy fighting. Saigon was relatively quiet for a few days thereafter, but then new assaults struck Cholon and the Phu Tho racetrack. The outnumbered and outgunned NVA troops fought fanatically; it took both jet strikes and repeated infantry assaults to dislodge the last of them from a slum near the 'Y' bridge.

By the 13th of May, it seemed the communists were finished in Saigon, leaving 5270 dead as compared to 154 Americans and 326 ARVN. But on 25 May the enemy was back in strength; the allies had to start from scratch in fighting for some of the same objectives. To the south, Vietcong units mounted a two-pronged attack on the Cholon district while the NVA struck the northern suburbs. It took three days of heavy fighting in early June, with support from planes, tanks, and helicopters, to clear the last pockets of resistance. For over five weeks thereafter, the communists sent dozens of rockets slamming daily into the city, hitting houses, streets, and gardens at random. Hundreds of

Above: *North Vietnamese man an anti-aircraft position. US aircraft losses in Southeast Asia totaled 8588 by 1973 – almost $7 billion worth of planes and helicopters.*

Top left: *A captured 75-mm weapon is examined by US Marines.*

Left: *An M-113 APC provides cover for men of the 9th Infantry Division during May 1968 fighting south of the 'Y' Bridge.*

Right: *Communist soldiers armed with Chinese- and Soviet-made weapons surprised in a hut.*

Top: *Ground fighters were quick to call in air support when they found themselves in trouble.*

Above: *Constructing a command post tent, to be transported on the back of an M577 command truck, near Tay Ninh.*

Left: *Troops scatter as a helicopter sweeps into a landing zone.*

civilians were killed, thousands wounded, thousands left homeless. The population of Saigon lived through those weeks in terror.

The Tet II attacks ran unpredictably into the autumn, right through the landmark date of 13 June 1968, when the Vietnam War became the longest in American history – more than 6-1/2 years to that date. In early August, allied forces went back to the Ashau Valley, where the communists had returned to rebuild a major staging area after being chased out in the spring. During the same period, NVA and VC forces struck 19 allied positions around South Vietnam; at Tayninh, American troops fought house-to-house for days to flush out the communists. A month later, the enemy was back at Tayninh in still greater force. With these grueling Tet II offensives, which flared over and over in the same places, the North Vietnamese were making their point: the war would grind on indefinitely until the United States pulled out.

US Offensives in 1969

When General Creighton W Abrams took over MACV command in the summer of 1968, he was expected to 'hold the fort until the Indians make peace,' as one United States officer put it. Abrams had to fight with steadily declining resources an enemy who seemed to be gaining strength all the time. In an effort to fulfill this frustrating assignment, the new commander reorganized his forces and rethought Vietnam strategy, giving greater priority to protecting Saigon and other major population centers. He favored relatively small operations by which to isolate enemy troop concentrations and hit them with everything he had – the 'cordon and pile-on' technique. To pursue this strategy, Abrams turned away from Westmoreland's emphasis on fixed strongpoints in the countryside and built up the airmobility of his forces.

The ultimate aim of the war under the Nixon administration was summarized in the new word 'Vietnamization': responsibility for the fighting was to be shifted gradually to the Army of the Republic of Vietnam; the South had to be ready to defend itself after the United States had pulled out.

Abrams began his offensives of 1969 with an American/ARVN drive to clear the VC from Cape Batangan in Quang Ngai Province. Then, at the end of January, came the eight-week Operation Dewey Canyon, in which the Marines struck an NVA logistical base just north of the always-troublesome Ashau Valley,

near the Laotian border. The operation ran into two weeks of steady downpour and strong enemy resistance. Finally, the rains stopped and air strikes could help the Marines; the enemy promptly withdrew into neutral Laos. In late February, the Marines had the frustrating experience of watching a stream of enemy trucks driving in plain sight on Route 922, just across the border. Acting on his own, Colonel Robert H Barrow took the risky step of ordering an ambush into Laos on Route 922. With some foreboding, Abrams approved. For over a week during late February, a Marine battalion fought in Laos, capturing an immense cache of enemy supplies. Dewey Canyon wound up by accounting for some 1617 communists killed; 130 Marines had died. But the fighting was far from over in the Ashau area.

After the 1969 Tet holiday, the communists shelled cities around the South again, concentrating on Saigon. A major test of Vietnamization came in early May, when 2000 NVA troops besieged a Special Forces camp at Benhet, near the Cambodian border. Inside were 250 American troops and 750 *montagnards*. The task of relieving the siege fell on South Vietnamese marines, who for several weeks fought actively around Benhet. But when the communists proved hard to discourage, the South Vietnamese troops began pulling back to their bases. What could have been a disastrous situation ended when the NVA besieging Benhet inexplicably pulled out in June. There

Left: *An Armored Personnel Carrier fights its way through dense undergrowth during a firefight near Long Binh: February 1969.*

Below left: *Marines share a moment of peace during a prayer service at Fire Support Base Razor early in 1969.*

Below: *The dependable Huey could carry 13 men into remote areas like this one near Bong Son, where members of the 173rd Airborne Brigade are setting up a perimeter.*

Far left: *XXIV Corps Fire Support Base on Hill 88 in Thua Thien Province.*

Left: *A mud-covered infantryman emerges from a firefight in a rice paddy.*

would be further tests of Vietnamization, but this early one was not encouraging.

When Operation Dewey Canyon wound up, a MACV report claimed that it had succeeded in 'effectively blocking the enemy's ability to strike out . . . to the east.' As so often before, however, that report proved to be overoptimistic. Within weeks, the communists were back in force in their old staging area around the Ashau Valley, where United States forces had fought bitterly in the Dewey Canyon and the Delaware/Lam Son operations. In mid-May 1969, American airborne and ARVN units headed back to the Ashau for Operation Apache Snow.

Allied troops unloaded from the helicopters and gathered into companies to hunt the NVA. At first, the enemy stayed out of sight, but after a day it became evident that an NVA regiment was dug in on Hill 937, named Dong Ap Bia, southwest of the Ashau on the Laotian border. An Army historian would observe later that Hill 937 was 'of no tactical significance. However, the fact that the enemy force was located there was of prime significance. . . . And so, the battle of Dong Ap Bia ensued.' It would become one of the most grueling and controversial of the war.

Lieutenant Colonel Weldon Honeycutt deployed his companies around the hill and called in air strikes. Next day the troops began working up the slopes, running into severe fire; the day after that, a three-pronged attack had no success, and the same pattern prevailed for the next several days. At some point the GIs bestowed on Dong Ap Bia the name by which history would remember it: Hamburger Hill, a grim indication of what enemy guns were doing to the attacking Americans.

A major assault on 18 May pushed close to the top of Hamburger Hill; at that point, however, rains turned the bombed out summit into a mudslide. But the offensive went on. 'That damned [Honeycutt] won't stop until he kills every damn one of us,' one soldier was heard to say. Reinforcements arrived, and on 20 May, after nine days of ghastly and heroic fighting, the top of Hamburger Hill was secured. A week later, it was abandoned.

Public response when the news reached the States was outrage: Senator Edward Kennedy called the battle 'senseless and irresponsible.' What, after all, had been accomplished at Hamburger hill? An NVA command post had been wiped out – temporarily – and 630 communists had been killed as compared to 56 Americans. Not much more could be said. In any event, after the battle Washington quietly told General Abrams to go easy on the ground fighting. Nixon did not want embarrassing American combat deaths to remind the public that there was still a full-scale war going on. Before the US withdrawal in 1973, some 8,744,000 American servicemen would have served in the war, of whom 47,253 would die in combat and another 10,449 would die in country. As the war ground on, growing numbers of eligible youth would avoid the draft by gaining student or occupational deferments, while an estimated quarter-million simply didn't register for the draft, in defiance of the law.

The Air War Continues

An overview of American air campaigns as they developed in 1965 would include Operation Farm Gate, the defoliant spraying of vast areas of the country; Operation Rolling Thunder over North Vietnam, carried on at first largely by F-105 Thunderchiefs, later by F-4 Phantoms and F-111 fighter-bombers; the Arc Light missions, flown by B-52s against communist positions in South Vietnam (to little effect); and the Operation Steel Tiger missions in Laos.

Over the years, the bombing of the North escalated. In 1967 US Air Force jets concentrated increasingly on the Hanoi-Haiphong areas, trying to cripple those major supply and logistical centers; inevitably, civilians were killed in the process. During 1967 the United States lost 328 planes over the North, many of them to deadly Soviet SAM (surface-to-air) missiles. The same year, 225 planes and some 500 helicopters were downed by enemy fire in the South.

President Johnson announced a partial halt to bombing of the North in March 1968, which helped bring Hanoi to the bargaining table, but the talks soon stalled and the raids resumed, now including B-52 strikes. When they finished in October 1968, United States planes had flown 117,000 Rolling Thunder missions, dropping over two-and-one-half-million tons of bombs and rockets – all to no discernible effect on the communist war effort. Just before the 1968 elections, Johnson announced a complete bombing halt in the North, in the futile hope of a breakthrough in negotiations; at the same time, there was a threefold increase in air strikes on the Ho Chi Minh Trail in Laos and heavy B-52 bombing continued in the South. (Throughout this period, air strikes remained an integral part of American ground operations.) However Johnson's hope of maximizing his chances for re-election by a gesture toward peacemaking were doomed to failure. Opportunists always, the

Above: *A Phantom releases Mk 84 laser-guided bombs over North Vietnam.*

Left: *Lt Randall H Cunningham, pilot, right, and radar intercept officer Lt jg William P Driscoll, were the first American fliers to qualify as aces solely as a result of Vietnam War action. Their aircraft is an F-4J Phantom II.*

Right: *The aircraft carrier* Enterprise *suffered a major fire in 1969, when a Zuni rocket on a Phantom was accidentally fired into planes on the tightly packed flight deck. Twenty-eight men were killed and 15 aircraft destroyed before the fire was brought under control.*

communists made good use of every bombing halt to step up their infiltration.

Richard Nixon came to the presidency in 1969 convinced that the best way to end the war quickly was to bomb the enemy into submission. His national security advisor, Henry Kissinger, was actively in agreement. Accordingly, soon after Nixon took office he ordered a series of B-52 raids called Operation Breakfast (usually known as the 'Menu' bombings). They were to fall on communist sanctuaries in neutral Cambodia, and were therefore kept secret from the public and from Congress. Mean-

Above: *An F-111A fighter-bomber equipped with terrain-following radar.*

Top right: *The 8th TFW, led by Col Robin Olds, was nicknamed the Wolfpack.*

Near right: *A MiG is hit by 20mm cannon fire from a USAF F-105.*

Far right above: *An OV-1B equipped with side-looking aerial radar.*

Far right below: *Its official task was reconnaissance, but the OV-1 Mohawk, manufactured by Grumman, also carried rockets, guns and napalm.*

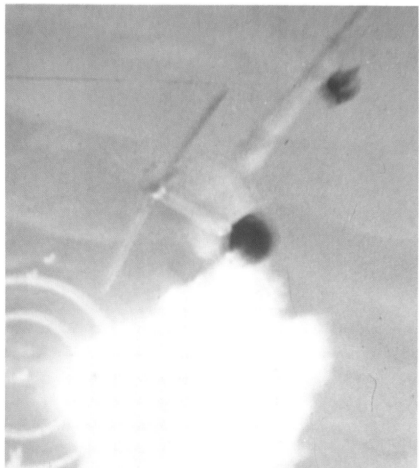

Above: *Marine F-4s in the maintenance area at Danang.*

Top right: *Operation Linebacker: Three Navy Phantoms and three A-7E Corsair II attack planes over North Vietnam.*

Right: *The HC-7 Seasprite was used for rescue operations.*

Left: *An AH-1G Cobra from the 71st Assault Helicopter Company, called the Rattlers.*

159

Above: *An A-6 Grumman Intruder on a combat mission from the carrier* Constellation. *The Intruder's main missions were all-weather and night attacks.*

Right: *A Skyhawk prepares to launch from the* Enterprise *as a Kaman H-2 Seasprite guard plane hovers above.*

Far right: *A member of Fleet Training Command instructs a South Vietnamese seaman in operation of the 20mm cannon.*

while, bombings in the South and in Laos were scaled up: in a 60 percent increase over 1968, nearly 160,000 tons of bombs were dropped on the Ho Chi Minh Trail in 1969 as part of that year's 242,000 bombing sorties.

With the secret bombing of Cambodia, Nixon began the process that would bring down his presidency: the bombings leaked to the *New York Times* in May. Outraged at the leak, Nixon and Kissinger ordered secret wiretaps on newsmen and officials, including some of Kissinger's own staff. The abuses of authority that would later climax at the Watergate building had begun the long slide that would be documented by the Pentagon Papers.

Vietnamization

When he inherited the war in Vietnam, Richard Nixon faced a dilemma: he would not give in to the communists and thereby become the first president to lose a war; at the same time, American opinion demanded some show of disengagement, at least a reduction in combat troops and casualties. Part of the Nixon/Kissinger solution to this dilemma was increased bombing. The other part was the idea dubbed Vietnamization: the South Vietnamese were to be equipped and trained to fight their war alone.

Vietnamization became operative in spring 1969, when Defense Secretary Melvin Laird asked Congress for $150 million to provide the Army of the Republic of South Vietnam with the best American weapons. At that point, the ARVN was the poor stepchild of the war: underequipped, poorly led, plagued by desertion, only occasionally equal to fighting the communists. Starting in mid-1969, the ARVN began to receive a flood of American materiel, including M16 automatics, Huey helicopters, tanks, and ships. At the same time, the American

command made mighty efforts to train the Vietnamese to operate their new weapons, to develop the logistical system and strategic know-how to utilize them efficiently, and to improve the quality of ARVN officers.

Here and there these efforts bore fruit, but on the whole the ARVN remained a shaky and vulnerable fighting force. The essential problem was the same one that plagued the entire war: Vietnamese were not Americans, their traditions were different, their experience with technology was still relatively recent. They could not be remade into a modern army in a few short years. It was the leaders in Hanoi who knew how to use

Vietnamese to fight in Vietnam. And it was not lost on American soldiers that the morale of the communists was consistently far higher than that of the ARVN: a US military joke summarized the tactics of some ARVN units as 'search and avoid.'

Nonetheless, the Nixon administration proceeded as if Vietnamization were working as planned. In the summer of 1969, Nixon gave the long-awaited word that troop withdrawals would begin; on 7 July, the first United States battalion pulled out. By the end of that year, some 60,000 personnel would be withdrawn. The fighting and dying, however, would continue for many months to come.

Above: *A member of the Civilian Irregular Defense Group (CIDG) moves carefully through dense vegetation.*

Near right: *A Vietnamese scout and his patrol leader check a map for their team's position.*

Top right: *Anti-war demonstrators at Harvard University prepare to take over University Hall: 9 April 1969.*

The War on the Home Front

By 1969 a substantial part of an entire generation of young people was actively against the war. Caught up in a counter-culture that stressed drugs and an unconventional life style, they had become alienated from their own country. As to the war, they chanted: 'Hell no, we won't go!' On society at large, the watchword was, 'Don't trust anyone over thirty.' On the campuses, demonstrations against the war turned into rage against all authority; in that era, the Students for a Democratic Society (SDS) and other radical groups occupied administrative buildings and shut down Columbia, Harvard, and a number of other universities. Outside the 1968 Democratic National Convention there had been a virtual war in the streets, with the Chicago police wrestling, beating, tear-gassing their way through 10,000 anti-war demonstrators.

A group called the 'Chicago Eight' was indicted for conspiracy to incite riot at the Democratic Convention. The defendants included a sampler of radical factions: hippie Jerry Rubin, 'Yippie' (Youth International Party) figure Abbie Hoffman, SDS leader Tom Hayden, and Black Panther Bobby Seale. (Seale was later given a separate trial and the defendants became the Chicago Seven.) The trial dragged on for months and became a circus, with the defendants dressing wildly and shouting obscenities at the judge while thousands of Yippies and SDS students demonstrated in the streets outside the courtroom.

In February 1970, all seven defendants were acquitted of incitement to riot; five were sentenced to jail on a related charge, but the convictions would be reversed. Seale was released on a mistrial. One of the Seven later observed, to no one's surprise, 'We were guilty as hell.' What had happened was that the judgment of jurors and public alike had gone against the United States government itself, for waging the war that led to the riots in Chicago. The inability of authorities to convict the Chicago Seven or to control their defiance in court showed that the war was also debilitating the justice system.

Nixon continued to withdraw troops through 1969, but it did not have the desired effect on public opinion. In November 250,000 people gathered in Washington for Vietnam Moratorium Day, the largest anti-war protest in American history. This time the demonstrators involved far more than student radicals: they included the distinguished economist John Kenneth Galbraith, labor leader Walter Reuther, even Republican Party chairman Roger Morton. Forty members of the House endorsed the Moratorium; 20,000 businessmen rallied in support on Wall Street; sister demonstrations were held around the country and the world. Some soldiers in Vietnam wore black armbands to show support. The anti-war movement now included some of those fighting the war.

Against the advice of Kissinger and his cabinet, Nixon characteristically stonewalled the Moratorium: 'Under no circumstances will I be affected whatever by it,' he proclaimed, and added that on the day of the march he planned to watch a football game on TV.

Spillover into Cambodia

In March of 1970, Cambodian Prince Norodom Sihanouk was overthrown by General Lon Nol. It was the end of Sihanouk's long struggle to maintain neutrality for his country; to try and find guarantees, he had tilted first toward China, then toward the United States, as the North Vietnamese and Vietcong increasingly used his country for staging areas. Finally, Sihanouk had given in to United States pressure and allowed bombing of communist sanctuaries in Cambodia. Meanwhile, the Cambodian economy was in shambles and the NVA was equipping and training an indigenous communist guerrilla army – the Khmer Rouge – who would later perpetrate one of the bloodiest genocidal campaigns in history.

Taking over a country in chaos, Lon Nol was helpless to do anything when Nixon decided to order troops across the border to strike communist sanctuaries. In May and June 1970, a force of 30,000 Americans and 48,000 ARVN, with extensive United States air support, operated against enemy bases in Cambodia. One American officer described the operation as, 'Pure blitzkrieg, something like a World War II Panzer division's book of tactics.'

By the time the allies pulled out of Cambodia, they had achieved considerable success, at least on paper: enormous quantities of war materiel and food had been seized, 11,349 communists were counted as killed, and the ARVN had fought impressively. However, a suspected major communist base in the so-called Fishhook area had not turned up, and many of the casualties proved to be civilian victims of bombing raids. And as usual, the enemy moved back in after the allies left.

As President Nixon had anticipated, protests flared after his announcement of the Cambodian invasion. They were more pervasive, violent, even tragic, than anyone could have expected. Not only did three of Kissinger's aides resign; 250 State Department employees joined many members of Congress in condemning the invasion. But what shocked the world was an

Left: *Prince Sihanouk of Cambodia gestures toward a display of weapons received from Communist China, during a visit by Chinese ambassador Cheng Shu-liung and Madame Cheng. Reportedly, 'neutral' Cambodia received almost enough military aid from its gigantic neighbor to equip its entire army.*

Top right: *Students at Kent State University, Ohio, flee tear gas released by National Guardsmen brought onto the campus to quell a massive anti-war protest on 7 May 1970. Moments later the Guardsmen fired into the crowd, killing four students and wounding several others.*

Right: *National Guardsmen in gas masks take aim on the Kent State campus.*

afternoon at Kent State University in Ohio, where a detachment of National Guardsmen were confronted by a jeering, rock-throwing group of student protesters. Feeling threatened, the Guardsmen suddenly wheeled and opened fire into the crowd. Ten people were wounded, four killed; two of the dead were passers-by. Within a week, 200 colleges and universities closed in protest strikes, many involving violent demonstrations. Washington was practically buried under mail condemning the Cambodian invasion and the tragic events at Kent State.

In the face of this explosion of rage and death, Nixon was defiant – and vindictive as well. He formed a covert team headed by a one-time Army intelligence man to spy on dissenters in and out of government. Now American militiamen had killed United States citizens and Americans were spying on their countrymen. The casualties of the war mounted everywhere.

The Deterioration of Military Morale

Far left: *A weary soldier shares a moment of sleep with his puppy at the Quang Tri staging base while awaiting airlift to a combat zone.*

Left: *A Saigon prostitute solicits an American soldier.*

Above: *Drug use, from marijuana to heroin, was epidemic among US servicemen in Vietnam in the latter stages of the war.*

Since everything to do with a war affects their lives intimately, soldiers are quick to pick up changes in the wind. It was clear enough in 1970 that the ground fighting was winding down, and that American public opinion was increasingly against the war. Soldiers returning home were often greeted by rage or silence, and word of that got back to 'Nam. The educational level of recruits was declining, and there were very few of the smart, idealistic young men who had once volunteered in hundreds. The soldiers coming in tended to be poor, uneducated, often black or Hispanic, plus a few college kids who hadn't succeeded in evading the draft. As for the communists, they seemed as strong and resilient as ever.

The results of this situation were predictable and inexorable. Alcohol and prostitutes are the traditional solaces of the soldier, and both were readily available in Vietnam. The new element was drugs, also readily available, cheap, and of high quality: dealers in marijuana, cocaine, speed, and heroin were everywhere in the cities. In 1971 a Defense Department study estimated that up to one-fourth of the lower-ranking troops were addicted to heroin.

In 1969, 9414 Americans died in Vietnam, down from the peak of 14,492 the previous year. Few saw this as a hopeful statistic. Soldiers dread being maimed or killed near the end of a war, especially a losing war. The term 'fragging' became familiar: it meant the murder by soldiers, often with fragmentation grenades, of officers who were too insistent on ordering their men to fight. In 1970, there were 209 incidents of fragging in which 34 officers were killed. The previous year had seen 117 convictions for mutiny or refusing to follow orders, compared to 82 in 1968. Racial incidents multiplied, with one black-white brawl aboard a Navy carrier leaving 46 injured. These signs of rage and despair escalated to the end.

The Drive into Laos

Early in 1971, MACV command began predicting (accurately, as it turned out) a communist buildup toward an offensive scheduled for the coming year. It was decided that an attempt must be made to forestall that offensive by cutting, once and for all, the Ho Chi Minh Trail in Laos – something that years of United States bombing had failed to do. The operation had to be an ARVN job, however; after the Cambodian invasion, Congress had forbidden United States ground troops to enter either Cambodia or Laos.

To prepare the incursion, ARVN and American units mounted Operation Dewey Canyon II in late January, reoccupying the area around Khesanh and massing at the Laotian border. Then, airlifted across the border by some 2600 American helicopters, the ARVN began Operation Lam Son 719 as United States jets and B-52s pounded targets in Laos.

President Thieu and his advisors had detailed some 30,000 men for the operation – half what the American command had suggested. Far larger than any previous ARVN ground campaign, the strike into Laos made slow progress due to severe resistance and poor logistics. The major objective was Tchepone, a town 200 miles inside the border. By the time the ARVN reached it, Tchepone had been leveled by United States air strikes. Nonetheless, the South Vietnamese were soon retreating under close NVA pursuit. Many soldiers panicked; the most enduring image of Lam Son 719 was photos of ARVN troops clinging desperately to the skids of American helicopters as they tried to bring out the wounded.

As usual, both sides claimed victory, the North Vietnamese ridiculing the ARVN and the South Vietnamese claiming they had closed the Ho Chi Minh Trail. In any event, the trail was soon back in operation. ARVN casualties in Lam Son 719 were estimated at an appalling 3800 dead, 5200 wounded, 775 missing – over a third of the entire force. Losses among United States support units were 405 dead, 104 helicopters downed, and 608 damaged. Although enemy operations had been set

Above: *Laotian soldiers respond to roll call. The 1971 incursion into Laos eroded public support of the war to a new low.*

Right: *South Vietnamese troops in Laos captured or destroyed some 7000 weapons, in addition to tanks, trucks, and munitions.*

back temporarily and many ARVN units had fought well, Lam Son 719 verged on a debacle – and was another ill omen for Nixon's policy of Vietnamization.

The Laos incursion brought renewed protests in the United States. As part of its continual erosion of Nixon's power to pursue the war, Congress had recently repealed the Gulf of Tonkin Resolution. Citing that fact, Senator Fulbright declared the incursion illegal. More ominously, a radical group called the Weather Underground exploded a bomb in the Capitol building. Beginning a week of massive demonstrations in Washington in late April, a new group called Vietnam Veterans Against the War littered the Capitol steps with combat ribbons and uniforms. The veterans called their protest 'Operation Dewey Canyon III.'

The Pentagon Papers

In 1967 Defense Secretary Robert McNamara had gathered a staff to compile all the governmental papers available relating to the Vietnam War. The study finally amounted to 47 volumes, covering the period 1945 to 1968. Between June and December 1971, that top-secret material turned up in the pages of the *New York Times* under the title 'The Pentagon Papers.' It was soon learned that the volumes had been leaked by Daniel Ellsberg, who had once been an idealistic pro-war assistant to McNamara. Having turned against the war with equal passion, Ellsberg determined to make the papers public. The results were explosive in several ways.

First, the papers themselves revealed years of confusion, bad judgment, coverups, and duplicity by government officials conducting the war: no one seemed to know exactly why the United States was in Vietnam and what its goals were, and there was a pervasive tendency to keep operations from public knowledge. Second, the Supreme Court denied Nixon's request to stop publication of the Pentagon Papers, citing freedom of the press. Third, since legal means had failed him, an enraged Nixon stepped up his covert war on leaks and dissent. 'I want to know who is behind this,' he fumed. 'I want results . . . whatever the costs.' With Kissinger's approval, Nixon formed a secret group within the White House to stop leaks; they called themselves jokingly 'the plumbers.' A list of some 200 purported enemies of the administration was drawn up by Nixon special counsel Charles Colson; the list included known leftists, anti-war leaders, and many journalists, but also people like actor Gregory Peck, football quarterback Joe Namath, and Harvard president Derek Bok. Said plumber Emil Krogh, 'Anyone who opposes us, we'll destroy.' Their efforts soon turned toward destroying Daniel Ellsberg; instead, they destroyed themselves and Nixon.

The Pentagon Papers added more fuel to the anti-war fire. Protesters began raiding draft offices, burning records and intelligence reports. The Senate voted in June to require a troop pullout by spring 1972; the House killed the proposal, but anti-war senators kept trying with increasing success.

Nixon was simultaneously stepping up bombing, pursuing negotiations, and pulling forces out. During 1971 the troop level dropped from 280,000 to 159,000; American casualties dropped to 1386 from the previous year's 4204. At the end of January, the president had tried to placate critics by revealing that Henry Kissinger was holding secret talks with Hanoi representatives in Paris. Like the public talks, however, the secret meetings were going nowhere.

Top right: *Former presidential aide John D Ehrlichmann testifies on the Ellsberg-Pentagon Papers case: 26 July 1973.*

Right: *Nixon strives to restore the government's credibility with troops in the field during a visit to Vietnam.*

Above: *Presidential Secretary Rose Mary Woods would face a Federal grand jury before the Pentagon Papers/Watergate controversy was over.*

Left: *Slander, pressure and bugging were only some of the charges incurred by the White House 'plumbers' after the secret Pentagon Papers were published over Nixon's objections. Here the Senate Watergate Committee confers on the case with chairman Sam Ervin, right. From left, Senators Howard Baker and Lowell Weicker; assistant counsels Terry Lenzer and Rufus Edmiston.*

Struggles Over the Firebases

During 1970–71, much of the communist war effort turned to small-scale attacks on ARVN and American firebases in South Vietnam – convenient and standing targets. The results of these fights were variable. In July 1970, Firebase Ripcord, an American airborne installation, had to be evacuated after weeks of NVA shelling killed 61 men. The same NVA unit then went on to force the evacuation of nearby ARVN Firebase O'Reilly. About a year later, however, South Vietnamese troops withstood a heavy siege of Firebase 6 in the Central Highlands; United States flyers dropped napalm and 7.5-ton bombs on some 6000 NVA around the base. ARVN Firebase Fuller was not so lucky that year. Despite the fact that American planes dropped 60 tons of bombs on attacking forces, the base had to be temporarily abandoned.

Commanders found firebase security deteriorating in 1971. The maze of wire and security devices that encircled them were not being installed properly, and artillery was not being shifted regularly to avoid becoming a fixed target. During a March attack on Firebase Charlie 2, near Khesanh, 29 men were killed by rockets, one of which scored a direct hit on a bunker where many defenders had gathered, rather than scattering according to instructions.

General Abrams insisted that the bases be secure and took steps to improve the situation. As a subordinate observed, 'The day is past when United States units will engage in bloody combat for reasons not clear to the United States public and the President.' In other words, American troops were to keep their heads down in the bases and wait it out.

Right: *Infantrymen at Firebase 14, near Kontum, fire mortars into an enemy artillery position.*

Bottom left: *Troops unload a CH-47 Chinook bringing needed supplies.*

Below: *Members of the 2nd Battalion, 5th Cavalry, fire a 105mm howitzer from Firebase Anna in 1970.*

War Rages in Laos and Cambodia

Supported and emboldened by the growing strength of the Hanoi regime, communist insurgents made steady gains in Laos and Cambodia during 1971–72. Their operations were abetted by the turmoil accompanying the spillover of the Vietnam War – the United States bombings and the inability of Lon Nol in Cambodia, and Souvanna Phouma in Laos, to control domestic unrest or the incursions of foreign troops. In early 1971, Lon Nol was incapacitated for some time by a stroke, further weakening the shaky power structure that had allowed both Vietnamese Communists and the Cambodian Khmer Rouge to gain substantial territory. Repeated ARVN incursions into Cambodia, in which the South Vietnamese fought in co-operation with Cambodian troops, did not improve the situation. At the end of the year, communists encircled the capital of Phnom Penh; despite massive ARVN and US attempts to dislodge them, they held firm. By the middle of 1972, communists controlled most of the border area near South Vietnam. Later, just before the ceasefire,

most of the Vietnamese Communists recrossed the border, leaving the fighting to the fanatical Khmer Rouge.

Hanoi was no respecter of neutrality, whether of Vietnamese villagers or of border countries. The communists hid behind whomever they needed. Thus the story of Laos in those years was similar to that of Cambodia: growing destabilization from the depredations of both sides in the Vietnam War, with a concomitant improvement in the position of native communist insurgents – in this case, the Pathet Lao. American forces had been active in Laos from the beginning. In addition to the bombing operations, a Thai unit and a 30,000-man irregular force had been organized by the CIA and operated with some success against the communists (although they had no more luck than anyone else against the Ho Chi Minh Trail). Souvanna Phouma began talks with the Pathet Lao in summer 1972, but they led nowhere. Both Laos and Cambodia were to be taken up in the slide toward communist victory in Southeast Asia.

Left: *Members of the 11th Armored Cavalry display a propaganda sign found in Cambodia during the summer of 1970. Increasing destabilization in Cambodia, which was caught between the warring sides in Vietnam, contributed to the eventual triumph of the indigenous Pathet Lao.*

Above: *A North Vietnamese photograph released on the 40th anniversary of the founding of the Vietnam Workers Party (15 January 1970). It was captioned, 'In spite of fierce US bombings, traffic in North Vietnam has been firmly maintained.'*

Left: *Laotian regular army troops on a training exercise north of their capital, Luang Prabang.*

175

The Air War Heats Up

As America pulled ground forces out of Vietnam and the ARVN pursued their operations with limited success, Nixon and Kissinger relied on bombing to keep the communists in check. Eventually, the B-52 became one of the primary bargaining chips in negotiations – the main vehicle for advancing Nixon's idea of 'peace with honor.' Thus American air raids escalated through 1971, striking targets all around the North. Meanwhile, Hanoi steadily improved its anti-aircraft and SAM (surface-to-air missile) defenses. Near the year's end, United States bombing began to approach the levels of the Rolling Thunder raids that had ended in 1968. Then, in January 1972, American jets made one-third as many strikes on the North as they had in all of 1971. Communist positions in the South were also pounded regularly; on 13 February, B-52s flew a record 19 missions in one day in striking the enemy near Kontum.

Frustrated by the lack of progress in negotiations, and with the onset of another communist offensive around Easter 1972, Nixon ordered Operation Linebacker: during four days in April, United States jets flew 225 sorties against enemy concentrations above and below the DMZ. On the 10th, B-52s bombed the North for the first time since 1967; on the 16th, the big bombers struck the major cities of Hanoi and Haiphong, flying alongside jet strikes. In the United States, opinion polls showed widespread support for Nixon's intensified air war. A few planes and pilots were being lost, but to many people that seemed better than the old body counts.

Left: *A US Navy A-7 pulls away from a strike on the Hai Duong railway bridge to North Vietnam in May 1972. One span of the bridge was destroyed entirely and another damaged and displaced.*

Right: *Flight deck crewmen aboard the nuclear-powered attack aircraft carrier USS* Enterprise *in the South China Sea.*

Left: *An F-4 armed with a Sparrow missile – 1971.*

Top: *The huge B-52 bomber takes off for a mission.*

Above: *A load of bombs destined for targets in Vietnam.*

The Easter Offensive

Ho Chi Minh died in September 1969. After the passing of their longtime leader and prime inspiration, the Hanoi leadership fought the war in a holding pattern for some time, taking no risks on a major offensive. Meanwhile, power struggles within the North Vietnamese Army resulted in the decline of General Vo Nguyen Giap and the rise of chief of staff General Van Tien Dung, who was the chief planner of a new offensive set for Easter 1972 – timed to influence United States elections.

That offensive broke out with co-ordinated attacks on bases and towns along the DMZ; some 150,000 NVA troops and thousands of Vietcong were involved. As with the 1968 Tet Offensive, MACV and ARVN commanders were taken by surprise (General Abrams was out of the country on vacation). A novel feature of this offensive was that the communists had received immense supplies of new Soviet equipment, including long-range heavy artillery and 500 tanks. Another contrast to previous outbreaks was that the ARVN would bear the brunt of allied fighting – with maximum American air support.

Within days, the well-equipped NVA swept across the DMZ and routed the ARVN 3rd Division. The goal of this drive was Quang Tri City, and after that, Hué. United States Operation Linebacker air raids soon geared up and slowed the offensive, but did not prevent the communists from opening new fronts in Binh Long Province near Saigon, and in the Central Highlands, where they surrounded the town of Anloc and trapped its ARVN defenders in a siege that would go on for two months.

With punishing US Air Force raids at their disposal, the ARVN 3rd Division pulled together and began picking off communist tanks with their new American LAW anti-tank weapons. By late April the offensive was at a standstill on all fronts, but then the bickering of ARVN commanders negated their gains and Quang Tri fell to the NVA, with the 3rd Division scattering in panic. In response, Nixon stepped up the air war again, to unprecedented levels. On 8 May he announced that all major North Vietnamese ports would be mined; almost immediately, a wave of violent anti-war protest surged across the United States, with echoes around the world.

In mid-May the ARVN began a counteroffensive with attacks on the communists at Quang Tri and Kontum; steadily widening its supporting air strikes, the United States devastated enemy supply lines and facilities. After weeks of bitter street-by-street fighting, the ARVN finally recaptured Quang Tri in mid-September, effectively ending the communist Easter Offensive. Battered and exhausted, the opposing forces settled down in place. In a bleak assessment, NVA leaders concluded that prospects of a quick military victory were gone, and that it would take years to build back up to a comparable campaign. For their part, the ARVN felt they had finally proven themselves, although it was clear to all that American air strikes had been indispensable.

Most depressing of all to Hanoi were the actions of its allies. The American air strikes had been the worst of the war, killing hundreds of North Vietnamese civilians, hitting hospitals and schools and the crucial dikes. (Contrary to Hanoi's charges, however, there seems to have been no deliberate American attempt to break the dikes, which would have devastated large areas). However, despite all the bombing, Nixon's 1972 overtures to the Russians and the Chinese met with extraordinary success – the president made a historic visit to China in February and had a summit conference in Moscow in May. Clearly, Hanoi's allies now felt that fence-mending with the United States was important.

Right: *Outnumbered South Vietnamese troops operate a tank against the April 1972 offensive aimed at Quang Tri City.*

Above: *North Vietnamese civilians view the wreckage of a USAF B-52 shot down over Hanoi in 1972.*

Right: *A Hanoi hospital heavily damaged by a B-52 bombing raid.*

Politics and Peace

During the second half of 1972, Nixon made his great attempt to break the North Vietnamese by bombing them into submission. After the gigantic Linebacker raids that followed the communist Easter Offensive came the 'Linebacker II' sorties over North Vietnam around Christmas 1972. In the most concentrated air offensive of the war, the United States Air Force dropped some 40,000 tons of bombs, mainly on the densely populated area between Hanoi and Haiphong. Pinpoint bombing – often using new laser- and television-guided 'smart' bombs – kept civilian casualties down, but they still totaled some 1318 in Hanoi and 305 in Haiphong; many more were injured. During the raids, the North Vietnamese shot down 26 American planes, including 15 B-52s.

At the same time, the American ground war was ending. In November the United States turned over its big base at Long Binh to the ARVN, symbolizing the end of this phase of American involvement. By the end of 1972, there were only 24,000 American servicemen left in Vietnam – although 4300 had been killed during the year. Perhaps because of the combat withdrawals, the Christmas bombings provoked little public outrage. The press, however, responded sharply: the *New York Times* called the raids 'Stone Age barbarism.'

Around the world, diplomats renewed their efforts to promote peace during the bombings of late 1972. In Paris, the formal talks had resumed in July after a break, but more promising were the secret talks between Henry Kissinger and Hanoi diplomat Le Duc Tho. With the presidential election imminent, Kissinger and North Vietnam announced in October that a ceasefire was near. Kissinger tried to strong-arm South Vietnamese President Nguyen Van Thieu into accepting the agreement, the White House ordered a bombing halt over the North, and Kissinger announced that the final ceasefire accord would definitely be signed on October 31.

Instead, the negotiations faltered: Thieu denounced the draft treaty, and Nixon backtracked. Nonetheless, the prospect of peace helped Nixon win re-election by a landslide; he carried all but one state over anti-war senator George McGovern. Soon after, Nixon ordered the Christmas bombings and minings, which seemed, in fact, to have helped bring Hanoi back to the table.

Scarcely noticed amid all the rumors of ceasefire and the election hoopla of 1972 was a strange event of 17 June: five men were arrested for breaking into the Democratic National Committee headquarters in Washington's Watergate complex. Only after the election would the ramifications of what a Nixon aide called that 'third-rate burglary' begin their long accumulation toward disaster for the Nixon administration. Nine days after the Watergate arrests, the Democratic National Convention Platform Committee announced that the first order of business would be immediate withdrawal of US forces from Vietnam.

The Last Push to a Ceasefire

Left: GIs stationed near Pleiku say goodbye to their South Vietnamese girl friends after the ceasefire signed in Paris on 27 January 1973.

Below: Vietnamese children near Duc Pho watch the departure of a US armored squadron.

Left: A member of the 443rd TFS displays the 'smart' bomb on his F-4.

The secret talks in Paris broke off just as the post-election bombings were about to begin, with each side accusing the other of intransigence. Following a Hanoi pledge to resume negotiations – and protests of the Christmas bombings from several European countries – Nixon called off air strikes above the 20th parallel on 30 December; the secret talks then resumed and made rapid progress.

On 27 January 1973, 'An Agreement Ending the War and Restoring Peace in Vietnam' was signed in Paris by the United States, North Vietnam, South Vietnam, and the Vietcong. President Thieu had finally given in to the inevitable, persuaded by massive last-minute American aid that had made the South Vietnamese Air Force the fourth largest in the world. Among the provisions of the settlement were a ceasefire set for 0800 hours on 28 January, Saigon time; withdrawal within two months of all remaining United States forces and dismantling of American bases; continuance of North Vietnamese Army troops in the South; and withdrawal of all foreign troops from Laos and Cambodia. (Laos would soon see a temporary ceasefire between government and Pathet Lao forces; in Cambodia, the fighting would continue, along with American bombings). Additional provisions maintained the DMZ at the 17th parallel pending reunification of Vietnam through 'peaceful means,' and promised that force would not be used to reunify the country.

Nixon proclaimed that 'We have finally achieved peace with honor.' Certainly, the agreement ended American fighting in the Vietnam War. But with respect to the future of the divided country, the accord was meaningless: North and South now gathered strength for the final struggle, which would last for two more years.

PART IV

The War Smolders On

A Fragile Ceasefire

For the United States, it was over except for the final withdrawal and the tallying of costs: 56,379 Americans dead, 306,653 wounded; 254,257 ARVN killed; nearly a million communists estimated dead; hundreds of thousands of Vietnamese civilians killed and half the population of South Vietnam left homeless; and some $139 billion expended (only World War II cost more). The incalculable social, political, medical, environmental, and spiritual repercussions of the war would unfold for decades to come.

As the last troops pulled out of Vietnam in late March 1973, ending ten years of US military presence, the details of disengagement went forward. At that point, the South Vietnamese government controlled about 75 percent of its territory and 85 percent of the population; the United States had given its allies enormous military aid and pledges of continuing support. Hanoi released the last of its acknowledged 587 American pri-

soners of war, who returned with stories of torture, heroism, and capitulation. During July, the Navy finished clearing American mines from North Vietnamese harbors. After repeated ceasefire violations by both sides following the original accord, the parties signed a new 14-point agreement in June, which proved as weak as the first in reducing hostilities.

Heavy United States bombing in Cambodia continued until August, when a Congressional cutoff of all military funds for Southeast Asia took effect. Congress, incensed by executive conduct of an undeclared war for 10 years, passed the War Powers Resolution over Nixon's veto in November 1973. It limited a president's ability to commit forces abroad without House and Senate approval. Nixon declared that the bill imposed 'unconstitutional and dangerous restrictions' on presidential authority, but dispassionate observers believed that executive authority had been too long abused.

Previous pages: *A South Vietnamese Marine guards a bunker complex near Quang Tri City as US forces withdraw from Vietnam.*

Above: *Long negotiations about the return of MIA crewmen shot down over North Vietnam, or their remains, followed upon the ceasefire with North Vietnam.*

Right: *Three Vietcong killed in an ambush by South Vietnamese militiamen six months after the ceasefire are exhibited by a roadside near Cu Chi.*

Above: *South Vietnamese war orphans play with 250lb bombs at a party given for them by US Marines (Airgroup 12) at Bien Hoa. The Marines were the last active US combat group to be based in Vietnam.*

Left: *Soldiers pass the time with a bridge game while waiting to be processed at Long Binh Junction.*

America's Postwar Trials

Drained and demoralized by the war, the American people wanted nothing so much as to forget about Vietnam entirely, but the inevitable aftershocks of war made this impossible. In 1974, Congress began cutting off aid to South Vietnam; by the following year it was a $300-million trickle. Despite countless pledges of continuing aid, the Thieu government was being left high and dry. Meanwhile, the communists geared up for the final push, but no one in America was ready to think about that.

President Nixon was not to be spared in the aftermath. In February 1973 the Senate established a Select Committee on Presidential Campaign Activities to investigate the Watergate break-in. In the months that followed, an extraordinarily sleazy story would unfold: connections between the Nixon re-election committee and the burglars who broke into the Watergate complex (to look for damaging information on Democratic candidates), and who had previously stolen records on Daniel Ellsberg from his psychiatrist; other illegal domestic spying, wiretapping, and sabotage of anti-war groups; widespread 'dirty tricks' against political opponents; and finally, a high-level coverup of all these crimes. At the same time, the Senate Armed Services Committee investigated the unauthorized secret bombings of Cambodia during 1969–70, finding the same pattern of covert activities, deception, and falsification of records.

Despite everything the Nixon administration could do to try and contain the investigation, the trail of indictments slowly climbed the ladder toward the Oval Office. First the Watergate burglars were tried, then their immediate superiors. Then Attorney General John Mitchell was indicted along with White House aides John Dean (who turned informer), H R Haldeman, and John D Erlichman. All were convicted and jailed. In the same period, Vice-President Spiro Agnew resigned and pleaded no contest to charges that he had received kickbacks while he was governor of Maryland. House minority leader Gerald R Ford was appointed to take Agnew's place.

On 27 July 1974, the Watergate scandal and coverup, and the secret bombing of Cambodia, finally arrived at Nixon's door. The House Judiciary Committee approved three articles of impeachment, charging the president with obstruction of jus-

Left: *Peter Rodino, chairman of the House Judiciary Committee impeachment inquiry, talks to John Dean, right, during a break in the proceedings of 12 July 1974. Dean testified that he and President Nixon had discussed the possibility of paying hush money to the Watergate defendants.*

Above: *USAF Capt William W Butler, returning from six years as a prisoner of war in North Vietnam, hugs his wife while their son embraces both of them in a joyful reunion: Travis Air Force Base, California, 18 March 1973.*

tice, violating his oath of office to uphold the law, and contempt of Congress. In the realization that his support in Congress was withering, Nixon became, on 8 August, the first president of the United States to resign. Clearly, he had engaged in unprecedented abuses of power while in office; equally clearly, the lingering rage of the government and the nation over the Vietnam War had played a major part in his downfall.

Gerald Ford, who became the country's first unelected president, quickly pardoned Nixon for any and all crimes. To charges of a 'deal,' Ford replied persuasively that the pardon was necessary to end the long national nightmare of Vietnam and Watergate. When the next election came, however, this act of clemency would play a major role in Ford's defeat.

Richard M Nixon boards a helicopter for the first leg of his flight to California after an emotional farewell to his White House staff: 9 August 1974. Upon his arrival in California, he became a private citizen, and Gerald Ford became president of the United States.

Below: *Flanked by his family, President Nixon delivers his resignation speech.*

The Final Campaign

When the parties involved signed the Paris agreements for the ceasefire, it is debatable if anyone really believed that Vietnam would ultimately be reunited by 'peaceful means,' as the accord stipulated. For the United States, it was a matter of signing a paper that would allow a relatively graceful exit. For the other signators, the ceasefire was a means of buying time for a military buildup. South Vietnamese President Thieu had no intention of coming to any agreement with the communists, and from the beginning, Hanoi had never seen reunification as coming about under any rule but its own.

During 1973 the communists expanded their logistics network – especially the Ho Chi Minh Trail – in preparation for the final offensive. Having moved thousands of troops and tons of supplies into the South by fall, they began small-scale raids on airfields, supply depots, and isolated outposts. President Thieu proclaimed in January 1974 that the war had 'restarted'; by March there was sustained and bloody fighting in the Central Highlands, and the communists had seized considerable territory in the Mekong Delta. Within a year of the 'ceasefire', 50,000 Vietnamese had died in the fighting. (Some 1,500,000 North and South Vietnamese died during the war.)

Hanoi began a probing offensive in January 1975. When Phuoc Long Province and its capital, Phuoc Binh – some 60 miles from Saigon – fell with surprising ease, communist commanders decided to mount a more aggressive campaign. In February, General Van Tien Dung arrived in the South to direct

Top left: *Operation Eagle Pull, Cambodia, 1975.*

Left: *Cambodian refugees disembark.*

Top and above: *Without the support of US money and personnel, the South Vietnamese war effort became progressively weaker until the inevitable collapse of 1975.*

the offensive; the following month, his forces took Ban Me Thuot in the Central Highlands. At that point, President Thieu very unwisely ordered ARVN units to abandon Pleiku and Kontum. The commander in that area promptly bolted and left his troops to their fate: only a third of the 60,000 soldiers made their way out. It was the beginning of a rout for the ARVN. Rivers of refugees, over a million people, flowed across the countryside, trying to escape the fighting and the communists. Everyone expected a bloodbath if Hanoi took over the South.

Before the oncoming enemy, the ARVN melted away, running with their families. Hué was abandoned, and Danang fell as frantic refugees fled to airports, docks, even into the sea. With the offensive making progress on all fronts, Hanoi ordered a push to Saigon before the rainy season in May. It was called the Ho Chi Minh Campaign.

By 8 April the communist advance had reached Xuan Loc, the last South Vietnamese defense line on the road to Saigon. There ARVN units fought desperately for two weeks while the enemy gathered around them. Then, running out of ammunition and tactical air support, the defending troops pulled back to Saigon and the communists converged on the capital from four directions. Everyone knew it was all over but the fleeing.

Below: Communist troops in Thailand go through training routines for the benefit of foreign journalists on the 13th anniversary of their initial deployment.

Right: A South Vietnamese trooper carries a wounded comrade during fighting near Kien Duc late in 1973.

Far right: A soldier mourns the death of a friend killed in a clash between South Vietnamese and communist forces in Chuong Thien Province, Mekong Delta: October 1973.

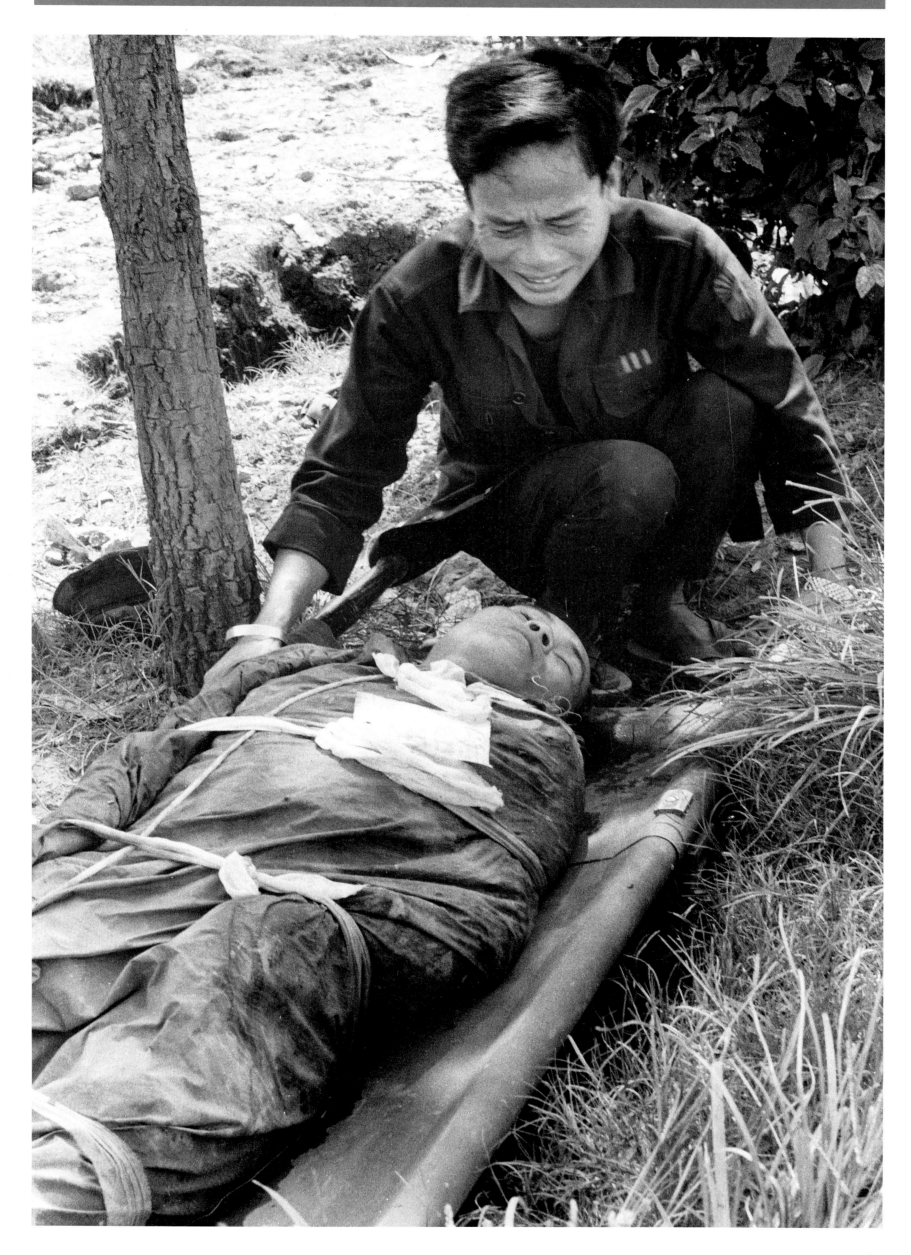

The Fall of Saigon

As the communists tightened the noose around Saigon, the chaos in the capital was indescribable – which is to say, the war ended the way of all wars for the losing side. With thousands of refugees surging through the city looking frantically for any way out, a fleet of 70 United States helicopters began shuttling back and forth in Operation Frequent Wind, the last United States operation in Vietnam. More than a thousand Americans and 6000 Vietnamese were evacuated from the city to offshore carriers. In previous weeks, some 50,000 Americans and Vietnamese had left.

President Thieu resigned on 21 April 1975 and fled the city a few days later, saying bitterly that the American failure to come to the aid of South Vietnam was 'an inhumane act by an inhumane ally.' The same week, President Gerald Ford announced calmly that 'Today, Americans can regain a sense of pride that existed before Vietnam. But it cannot be achieved by refighting a war that is finished. . . . These events, tragic as they are, portend neither the end of the world nor of America's leadership in the world.'

The final scenes of the long drama, on 29–30 April, were unforgettable: helicopters landing on the roof of the United States Embassy chancery, lines of terrified evacuees waiting to be airlifted, thousands of desperate citizens surrounding the compound begging to be rescued and kept at bay by rifles and bayonets. Ambassador Graham Martin, clutching an American flag, left on one of the last helicopters. On the evening of the 29th, communist infantry and tanks began pouring into Saigon with little opposition from the last ARVN units.

General Duong Van Minh, who had ordered the assassination of president Diem a decade before, ended up as nominal head of the South Vietnamese government. It was he who surrendered to NVA Colonel Bui Tin, whose armoured unit had first reached the presidential palace. Bui Tin recited: 'You have nothing to fear. Between Vietnamese, there are no victors and no vanquished. Only the Americans have been beaten . . . . The war for our country is over.'

On 7 May President Ford issued a statement proclaiming the end of the 'Vietnam era.' That same day, 30,000 people celebrated the communist victory in the streets of Saigon, soon to be renamed Ho Chi Minh City. The dream of independence and reunification that had fired Ho Chi Minh more than 60 years before had come to fruition.

Top left: *Last-minute evacuation of US Embassy personnel and civilians from the roof of the embassy – 29 April 1975.*

Top right: *South Vietnamese refugees arrived aboard the USS* Blue Ridge *in such numbers that their helicopter transports had to be pushed into the sea to make room for more to land.*

Right: *An Air America (CIA) helicopter prepares to land on the deck of the* Blue Ridge *during South Vietnamese refugee evacuations of 28 April 1975. In the background is the guided missile light cruiser USS* Oklahoma City.

Above: *South Vietnamese civilians leave the US commissary at Newport, outside Saigon, with goods salvaged when the commissary shut down in April 1975.*

Right: *The horrifying picture showing the feet of a South Vietnamese soldier protruding from the wheel-well of a refugee plane damaged upon takeoff from Danang Airbase. His desperate attempt to escape resulted in his death, and his mangled body was extracted from the plane when it landed in Saigon.*

The Collapse of Cambodia and Laos

Increasingly through the 1960s and early 1970s, the neutral border countries of Cambodia and Laos had become entangled in the Vietnam War; in the end, their fate was to be determined by the communist victory in Vietnam. In the same week of mid-April 1975 that Saigon was surrounded, the Lon Nol government in Cambodia surrendered to the Khmer Rouge, who had launched their final drive to victory from the foundation of territory seized by the North Vietnamese Army. Under their leader Pol Pot (born Salot Sar), the Khmer Rouge would mount a campaign of terror and murder against the population of their own country that has few parallels in history. In an attempt to create some kind of agricultural utopia, the Khmer Rouge murdered most of the educated citizens, drove urban dwellers into the countryside to work at forced labor, destroyed books and temples in an effort to erase the past, and by 1978 had killed an estimated two million people. That year, a Vietnamese invasion ousted Pol Pot and installed a Vietnamese-backed government – the People's Republic of Kampuchea.

In Laos, the government of Prince Souvanna Phouma and the communist Pathet Lao reached a tenuous agreement on a coalition government in 1974, after more than 20 years of fighting. When the communists took Saigon in April 1975, the coalition in Laos began to come apart. Fighting broke out, with North Vietnamese troops supporting the Pathet Lao. By December, the communists controlled most of the country. The Pathet Lao then abolished the coalition government, ended the 600-year-old monarchy, and proclaimed the People's Democratic Republic of Laos.

Thailand, an ally who had fought with the United States throughout the war, ordered the United States to close all its military bases in the country in March 1976. Only a small contingent of American military advisors would remain.

Left: *The infamous Pol Pot, leader of the Khmer Rouge, which murdered some 2 million Cambodians.*

Below: *Khmer Rouge guerrillas trek through the forest near the Thai-Cambodia frontier, scene of fierce fighting between the Cambodian communists and the Vietnamese communists – 1983.*

The *Mayaguez* Incident

One of the smaller but more spectacular aftereffects of the war came in mid-May 1975, when the Cambodian Khmer Rouge seized the United States cargo vessel *Mayaguez* in the Gulf of Siam with the claim that the ship was on a spying mission. President Ford immediately ordered a Marine battalion in Thailand to mount a rescue of the crew, who were believed to be captives on Koh Tang Island (in fact, they were being held at the port of Kompong Som). The ensuing operation verged on a Laurel and Hardy escapade, although the outcome was scarcely comic.

Following air strikes that sank three Cambodian gunboats in the area, a detachment of Marines landed on a destroyer and then stormed the *Mayaguez* – only to find it empty. Another detachment headed for Koh Tang in two wings; the island defenses erupted, downing 2 United States helicopters before they could land and killing 13 Marines. West of the island, two more helicopters were riddled, one of them escaping back to Thailand and the other falling into the surf after releasing its troops. Other helicopters landed safely.

The trouble was that the captives had never been on the island, and, moreover, had already been released by that time and were heading back to the *Mayaguez*. Before the news was received, the United States bombed several targets in Cambodia. It took 200 more Marines and massive bombing to get the original contingent of Marines off Koh Tang. Total United States casualties in the operation were 41, 23 of whom died in a helicopter crash in Thailand. Nonetheless, President Ford portrayed this inglorious episode as something that had restored American honor after Vietnam, and the nation seemed ready to believe it.

Above: *US Marines board the* Mayaguez *in the Gulf of Thailand in June 1975.*

Right: *Marines equipped with gas masks search the* Mayaguez.

Vietnam Turns on Cambodia, China on Vietnam

The genocidal holocaust in Cambodia raged from 1975 to 1978, during which time the Khmer Rouge broke relations with their former Vietnamese Communist allies after repeated border clashes. By the beginning of 1978, Vietnamese forces occupied some 400 miles of Cambodian territory along the border. Despite the manifest crimes of the Khmer Rouge, China backed Cambodia.

In December 1978, Hanoi began the well-planned lightning invasion of southern Cambodia that toppled the capital of Phnom Penh and overthrew the murderous government of Pol Pot. He escaped with some 40,000 Khmer Rouge, and the Vietnamese would operate with little success against the guerrillas in the years to come. Meanwhile, a Hanoi-backed puppet government took the reins of power in devastated Cambodia, and renamed it the People's Republic of Kampuchea.

The Chinese and Vietnamese had been enemies for the better part of two millennia, at least since the Han Dynasty burned the capital of Nam Viet in 111 BC. Their alliance under the banner of international communism during the war against the French and Americans was only a brief interlude of co-operation in a long history of enmity. Even during that time, Hanoi had felt betrayed by the Chinese both in the Geneva talks of the 1950s and in China's *rapprochement* with Nixon in 1972.

These long-standing resentments produced a progressive heightening of tensions after the war. When the Hanoi govern-

Top: *Vietnamese 'boat people' suffered incredible hardships in their flight from the communist takeover in South Vietnam.*

Right: *Refuges in the South China Sea prepare to board the amphibious cargo ship USS Durham for passage to a safe zone.*

ment nationalized privately owned businesses in Saigon (or Ho Chi Minh City) in 1978, hundreds of ethnic Chinese fled; Beijing then accused Hanoi – with good reason – of systematically abusing and expelling up to 90,000 Chinese since 1977. Soon the Chinese capital stopped all economic aid to Vietnam and withdrew its ambassador. Talks between the two countries failed, as China lambasted the Vietnamese for violating the borders of both Cambodia and China. When Hanoi signed a mutual aid and friendship pact with the Soviet Union, China branded the agreement a 'threat to the security' of Southeast Asia and began rattling the saber.

Finally, in February 1979, up to 300,000 Chinese troops pushed across the border, supported by air and artillery strikes: Beijing had mounted a major invasion of its erstwhile ally. However, after meeting stiff resistance that killed more than 20,000 of the invading troops, and receiving a stern warning from Moscow, China pulled back. Ensuing peace talks stalled when Beijing demanded that Hanoi pull all troops from Laos and Cambodia, and the two countries settled into the same rancorous standoff that had prevailed for centuries.

Above: *A Marine CH-53 comes in for a landing near Phnom Penh, Cambodia, for evacuation exercises: 12 April 1975, Operation Eagle Pull.*

Right: *Vietnamese communist soldiers operate an anti-tank rocket launcher in a border skirmish of 1982.*

Top right: *Vietnamese children watch American newsmen and civilians board a bus that will take them to an evacuation site in 1979.*

Refugees and Boat People

During the final communist victory in Southeast Asia, and in the months and years thereafter, hundreds of thousands of refugees poured out of the area, burdening surrounding nations and the United States. America had mounted major evacuations by air and sea even before Saigon fell. Soon after that, Congress appropriated $405 million for a refugee aid program and authorized some South Vietnamese and Cambodians to settle in the United States. Within months, 140,000 had arrived in the country.

Hanoi's National Assembly proclaimed the official unification of the Socialist Republic of Vietnam in 1976. The often-predicted bloodbath visited on former enemies never took place. Nonetheless, life was far from easy for the conquered; some 400,000 former South Vietnamese government and military people were sentenced to 're-education' camps, from which up to a quarter never emerged. Young men were conscripted in thousands to fight in Cambodia and Laos and along the Chinese border. Many former Vietcong felt that the North Vietnamese were cavalierly dominating the South. And in general, the Hanoi leadership, which had brilliantly defeated France and the United States, proved far less capable in coping with the demands of building a peacetime economy: the Vietnamese were great fighters, but poor governors. The country sank into stagnant poverty and was rife with the same kind of corruption that had prevailed before the communist victory.

As the Vietnamese economy foundered and the holocaust in Cambodia unfolded, the stream of refugees began to swell in 1977, with many putting out to sea in overcrowded, leaky vessels: thousands of these 'boat people' drowned, others were killed or turned back when they tried to land in neighboring countries. President Jimmy Carter tried to help the situation in the fall of 1977, easing the way for refugees to apply for United States citizenship and extending federal aid programs. At a Geneva conference in mid-1979, it was estimated that 300,000 people had fled Vietnam, Cambodia, and Laos during the year. By 1984 some 300,000 Southeast Asians had settled in the United States, but hundreds of thousands languished in grim refugee camps in Thailand, Cambodia, and Laos, and still more groups of boat people arrived regularly.

Another, perhaps even more tragic, group comprised the thousands of children in Vietnam who had been fathered by American servicemen. Hated by a xenophobic society, these children were abandoned, neglected, and often brutalized. American attempts to bring 8000 of them to the United States were stalled by Hanoi; the same tactics stymied efforts to discover the fate of Americans missing in action (MIAs), some of whom were rumored to be alive in Vietnam. Thus, year after year, the war continued to claim its victims.

The Legacy of the Vietnam War

Right: *The mute testimony of the Vietnam War Memorial in Washington, DC, bearing the names of 57,939 US soldiers killed or missing in action. Designed by Yale architecture student Maya Ying Li, it consists of two black granite walls forming a V and carries no inscription that identifies the war.*

Right: *A scene from Francis Ford Coppola's epic war film* Apocalypse Now, *released in 1979, which starred Marlon Brando, Robert Duvall and Martin Sheen.*

Bottom right: *Robert DiNiro and John Savage cling to the skids of a helicopter in the 1978 film* The Deer Hunter.

The human costs of the war would be paid through generations. As Henry Kissinger wrote some time later, 'Vietnam is still with us. It has created doubts about American judgment, about American credibility, about American power. . . . It has poisoned our domestic debate. So we paid an exorbitant price for the decisions that were made in good faith and for good purpose.'

Among veterans, the legacy often included drug addiction and post-combat psychological disorders, bringing in their wake divorce, crime, alcoholism, and suicide. Thousands had been exposed to the herbicide Agent Orange and faced the threat or fear of cancer and other diseases. In the nation at large, there was a new sense of suspicion toward government and especially toward the executive – Johnson, Nixon, Ford, and Carter were all in some degree damaged by the war's devaluation of the presidency and by Watergate. The military had been compromised as well; it would take years for the armed forces to regain a position of general respect and their share of high-quality recruits. And it is arguable that it was mainly the specter of Vietnam that kept President Ronald Reagan out of military involvement in Nicaragua and other areas of unrest.

The United States government did its best to contribute to the process of healing. Immediately upon taking office, President Jimmy Carter pardoned most of the 10,000 draft evaders of the war years, many of whom had fled to Canada and other countries. In 1982 the Vietnam War Memorial was dedicated in Washington, DC. Designed by Chinese-American Yale student Maya Ying Li, it is unlike any other war memorial, with no grandiose statuary, no inscription even identifying the war. It is simply two converging walls of black granite on which are inscribed the names of all the Americans killed or missing in Vietnam. Initially much criticized, the memorial came to be recognized as an eloquent testimony: the names of the dead for remembrance, with no attempt to gloss over the ambiguities of the war. On Veterans Day 1984, a statue was dedicated at the War Memorial – three infantrymen in field gear, looking uncertain and afraid. Slowly, the Vietnam Memorial became a focus of healing and of meditation on the nation's most troubling war and those who fought and died in it.

Perhaps movies, more than anything else, reflect how the nation has worked out its attitudes toward the Vietnam War. John Wayne tried to make it an old-fashioned heroic thrashing

Left: *A group of Amerasian children – some of the thousands fathered by US soldiers during the war – photographed in Vietnam in 1981.*

Above: *Dedication of the Vietnam Veterans' Memorial, 13 November 1982.*

Top left: *A Vietnam veteran keeps a 61-day fast and vigil in a bamboo cage on behalf of the men still missing in action from his home state of Washington.*

of the commies in *The Green Berets*; even in 1968, few members of the public were willing to buy that. Postwar movies such as *The Deer Hunter* and *Apocalypse Now* were powerfully made, but seemed to view the war primarily as a matter of innocent American boys sinking into a nightmare induced by the cruel and mysterious East. *The Killing Fields* was a stunning portrayal of the Cambodian holocaust, a chilling examination of how civilization can suddenly collapse into savagery.

Finally, in films like *Platoon*, *Full Metal Jacket*, and *Hamburger Hill*, the nation seemed to arrive at some consensus of feeling about the Vietnam War. It was seen as a tragedy on a vast scale and one of almost Shakespearean unfolding, defying easy dichotomies of good and evil. Those involved set off on a path of which they could not see the end, and which in its tortuous course destroyed the guilty and the innocent alike. They deserve our sorrow, our pity, and our respect.

Left: *President Ronald Reagan, Defense Secretary Caspar Weinberger (left), and Maj Gen John L Ballentine, watch the casket of the unknown soldier from the Vietnam War placed in the Tomb of the Unknown Soldier.*